Academic Writing for Interna
Students of Science

This revised and updated second edition is an accessible companion designed to help science and technology students develop the knowledge, skills and strategies needed to produce clear and coherent academic writing in their university assignments.

Using authentic texts to explore the nature of scientific writing, the book covers key areas such as scientific style, effective sentence and paragraph structure, and coherence in texts and arguments. Throughout the book, a range of tasks offers the opportunity to put theory into practice. The explorative tasks allow you to see how language works in a real scientific context, practice and review tasks consolidate learning and help you to develop your own writing skills, and reflective tasks encourage you to think about your own knowledge and experience, and bring this to bear on your own writing journey at university.

Key features of the new edition include:

- Updated content and additional tasks throughout
- New chapters, covering writing in the sciences and writing at university
- The introduction of reflective tasks
- Up-to-date examples of authentic scientific writing

Clear, engaging and easy-to-use, this is an invaluable tool for the busy science or technology student looking to improve their writing and reach their full academic potential.

Jane Bottomley is a lecturer in Engineering Communication at Kungliga Tekniska Högskolan (KTH), Sweden. She has worked as a writer, editor and lexicographer on a number of books, websites and dictionaries.

Academic Writing for International Students of Science

Second edition

Jane Bottomley

Routledge
Taylor & Francis Group

LONDON AND NEW YORK

Second edition published 2022
by Routledge
2 Park Square, Milton Park, Abingdon, Oxon, OX14 4RN

and by Routledge
605 Third Avenue, New York, NY 10158

Routledge is an imprint of the Taylor & Francis Group, an informa business

© 2022 Jane Bottomley

First edition published by Routledge 2015

British Library Cataloguing-in-Publication Data
A catalogue record for this book is available from the British Library

Library of Congress Cataloging-in-Publication Data
Names: Bottomley, Jane., author.
Title: Academic writing for international students of science /
    Jane Bottomley.
Description: Second Edition. | New York : Routledge, 2022. |
    "First edition published by Routledge 2015"—T.p. verso. |
    Includes bibliographical references and index.
Identifiers: LCCN 2021018199 (print) | LCCN 2021018200 (ebook) |
    ISBN 9780367632717 (Hardback) | ISBN 9780367632724
    (Paperback) | ISBN 9781003118572 (eBook)
Subjects: LCSH: Technical writing. | Communication in science. |
    Academic writing. | English language—Study and teaching—
    Foreign speakers.
Classification: LCC T11 .B667 2022 (print) | LCC T11 (ebook) |
    DDC 808.06/65—dc23
LC record available at https://lccn.loc.gov/2021018199
LC ebook record available at https://lccn.loc.gov/2021018200

ISBN: 978-0-367-63271-7 (hbk)
ISBN: 978-0-367-63272-4 (pbk)
ISBN: 978-1-003-11857-2 (ebk)

DOI: 10.4324/9781003118572

Typeset in Galliard
by Apex CoVantage, LLC

Contents

Acknowledgements   vi

Introduction to the second edition   1

1   **Writing in the sciences**   6

2   **Writing at university**   20

3   **Scientific style**   36

4   **Sentence structure 1**   56

5   **Sentence structure 2**   73

6   **Paragraph development: Achieving flow**   89

7   **Referring to sources**   103

8   **Writing coherent texts and arguments**   122

9   **Academic and scientific conventions**   142

Appendix 1: verb forms and patterns   163
Appendix 2: noun phrases   168
Appendix 3: common areas of difficulty in grammar and punctuation   176
Appendix 4: model texts   180
Answer key   186
Index   212

Acknowledgements

My thanks to the many students and colleagues who make teaching and writing so interesting and enjoyable. I would also like to thank all the fine writers whose essays, reports, dissertations, patents, articles, books and blogs I have drawn on to help others learn how you do what you do so well. That includes the students, skilled writers all, who very generously allowed me to use their work in progress in this book: Sarmed A. Salih; Astone Nanja; Parikshit Deshmukh; Jing Yan; Amani Jaafer. I am also grateful to Victoria Konstantinidi for her keen interest, and helpful ideas on the learner's perspective.

Particular thanks are owed to the following: Michael Burton, cousin and chemist, for his invaluable support and sound advice; John Morley and Vanesa Rodriguez Juiz for their feedback on manuscripts at various stages; and John Speller, at the University of Lodz, for his helpful comments on the first edition and for helping me to feel part of a wider community of scientific writing professionals.

Introduction to the second edition

Academic writing for international students of science is designed to help you, as a science and technology student at university, develop the knowledge, skills, tools and strategies needed to produce clear, coherent writing in assignments. It is aimed at students near the start of their scientific writing journey (in English), for example, about to start their first degree in English, or those studying on a pre-sessional course. But it may also be of interest to more experienced writers who want to brush up on their English language skills for academic purposes. It is aimed particularly at those for whom English is a second language, as the English needed in academic settings is, in some important respects, different from the English used in most other settings. The book covers science subjects as defined by the *International Standard Classification of Education* (ISCED): life sciences, physical sciences, mathematics and computing. It also includes medicine and healthcare, together with engineering. As well as writing, the book touches on reading and other skills, as it is not possible or desirable to look at one skill in complete isolation.

Accessibility and authenticity

There are many challenges facing you as you embark on your scientific studies. You need to assimilate a great deal of information, and engage in new ideas and intellectual processes. For this reason, you will no doubt be looking for study aids and resources that are accessible, i.e. easy to read and use. The language and organisational features of this book are geared towards creating an accessible resource, one which can complement the rest of your studies, rather than becoming an extra burden.

One of the key features of this book is the exploration of scientific language and discourse features using authentic examples of scientific writing. The texts under discussion have been selected because they are clearly written and demonstrate useful features, while also being accessible to students from a range of scientific backgrounds.

DOI: 10.4324/9781003118572-1

The book's approach and features

The first edition of this book emerged out of my teaching at the University of Manchester, in the UK, where I worked with students, including many international students and science students, to help them develop their academic skills. I now work with students at KTH, in Stockholm, with a focus on engineering English.

There are some general ideas which underpin the book.

- Firstly, it takes time and effort to get better at writing. This process will involve, among other things, exploring, reflecting, practising, experimenting, revisiting, recycling and responding to feedback.
- Secondly, writing can be both a joy and a struggle. There is the joy of finding the right word or crafting a good sentence, the satisfaction of finally getting a text to hang together with a clear thread of sense and meaning. There is also the struggle. Writing is often hard! But this is no bad thing really. Studying at university should be a transformative experience, and the struggle that comes with difficult learning processes is a necessary and enriching part of this.
- Thirdly, writing involves both the 'macro' level, i.e. the writing process itself, and broad issues such as clarity and coherence in writing, and the 'micro' level, i.e. the mechanics of writing such as grammar and punctuation. These two levels are interdependent and intertwine in many interesting ways.

The particular approach in much of the book takes the form of critical analysis of language and discourse in scientific texts. **Language** comprises elements such as words, phrases, grammar and punctuation. **Discourse** refers to the various forms of written or spoken communication associated with a particular academic discipline. In simple terms, the approach is based on the idea of *noticing* two very important things:

- what writers *do* in texts
- what language and discourse features they use to do it

This is accomplished largely through the **Explorative Tasks** which occur throughout the book. These help you to explore language and discourse in scientific writing, guiding you towards noticing important features associated with the communication of knowledge in the sciences. This explorative approach is rooted in constructivist, discovery-oriented learning theories, and the idea that discovering and working out things for yourself, often with hints and questions to guide you, can help you to assimilate knowledge. There are also **Practice Tasks**, which help you to further your understanding of different features of language and discourse, manipulate them in other contexts and think about how you might apply them to your own writing. **Review Tasks** allow you to revise points covered in a freer way by creating your own short texts.

When answers to tasks are provided in the **Answer Key**, this symbol is used:

Sometimes answers are included within a chapter immediately after the task, like this:

As mentioned, for some tasks, you are encouraged to produce a text. If you are using this book in class, you may be able to get feedback on your text from other students or a teacher. If you are using this book for self-study, **Model Texts** illustrate a possible response, and exemplify some language and discourse features that you may be able to adapt for your own use. If you are using this book on a course, your teacher may also refer to these texts for further analysis.

The book also includes a number of **Study Boxes** like this:

STUDY BOX

These provide guidance to help you complete the various tasks, as well as highlighting key language points and study strategies.

The book works as both a textbook that you can work through chapter by chapter, and as a reference that you can dip into when you want to focus on a particular area or need a particular piece of information.

The symbol

▶

refers you to related areas in other chapters and in the appendices.

The flag symbol alerts you to key points to note in a particular area of study:

New to the second edition

- **A new chapter on *Writing in science*.** I hope that this chapter will stimulate an interest in scientific communication in general and perhaps help to discourage a narrow view of writing, i.e. as confined to something that is only done to pass assignments – although this is of course one important consideration! The chapter discusses university writing as part of a wider consideration of writing in the sciences, including that which is connected to commercial endeavours and popular science. It is interesting to note that today, an academic in a university science department may find themselves writing a textbook for university undergraduates, a research paper for an academic journal, an article in a publication like *The Conversation*, to explain their research to non-experts, a popular science book, article or blog for the general public, or a patent application to transform their research into a commercial product. They may write some of these individually, and some in collaboration with colleagues. This could be alongside oral media output such as lectures, podcasts, videos and TV. You, as a science student, may or may not go on to produce such a wide variety of texts, but you will certainly read and access some or all of them, so it is well worth getting a sense of this bigger picture. This exposure and discussion may also, I hope, help you to develop your engagement with, and enjoyment of, a wide range of writing on science.

- **A new chapter on *Writing at university*.** This expands on the original chapter on the writing process in the first edition. It encourages you to reflect on your own feelings about writing and your experiences. It discusses your place in the university writing community, and addresses important issues such as responding to feedback and finding support, and even how you might become a happier writer! It then guides you through the different stages of the writing process, from initial analysis of an assignment, to final proofreading of the text.

- New **Reflective Tasks**. These invite you to think about your own knowledge, experience and understanding, and guide you towards finding out the things you need to know for future development.

- More **authentic examples of scientific writing**. Many readers have commented positively on the fact that language and discourse features are explored and exemplified through authentic scientific texts, and I have attempted to build on this in this new edition.

- More **examples illustrating language points**. Some readers commented that some grammatical explanations would benefit from more exemplification. I hope the examples added in this new edition will make these grammatical explanations easier to understand.

- New **content** and additional **tasks** throughout the book.

Please send any comments you have on the book to jabo@kth.se. I am always happy to receive your feedback and to continue to learn from it.

Jane Bottomley, 2021

References

The Conversation. Available at: https://theconversation.com/uk (accessed 2nd March, 2021).

ISCED. Available at: https://web.archive.org/web/20170326010815/https://uis.unesco.org/en/topic/international-standard-classification-education-isced/ (accessed 8th January, 2021).

CHAPTER 1

Writing in the sciences

In this chapter, we will explore writing in the sciences from a broad perspective. We will discuss the distinction between 'science writing' and 'scientific writing', and analyse examples from each category. We will identify the distinctive features of these texts in terms of their purpose, their audience (or readership), the language they use and the conventions they follow. These are concepts which will be discussed in relation to your own writing in subsequent chapters.

1 Scientists as communicators

Many claim that, for scientists, communication skills are almost, if not equally, as important as technical skills. According to Mónica I. Feliú-Mójer, writing in *Scientific American*, "to be a successful scientist, you must be a successful communicator" (2015). We can relate this sentiment to the growing mission of universities to forge strong links with wider society and to communicate research to the public in an effective way. See, for example, an initiative at my own university, KTH in Stockholm, where a research group is working to integrate communication training into postgraduate education "to sharpen the researchers' communication skills" (Gullers, 2020).

It is therefore important for you, as a science student, to possess a general understanding of the many different ways in which scientists and other interested parties communicate with each other and with the general public.

2 Terminology: 'scientific' writing or 'science' writing?

The term 'scientific writing' is usually reserved for the highly technical writing produced "by scientists for other scientists" (Hofmann, 2019: 10), with the word 'technical' meaning 'specific to a particular discipline'. We might also describe this type of writing as 'academic writing in the sciences'.

DOI: 10.4324/9781003118572-2

One of the most common and important forms of scientific writing is the peer-reviewed journal article reporting on primary research. At university, undergraduate and Master's science students will produce scientific writing for assessment purposes in the form of essays, reports, reviews and dissertations. PhD students will write theses and may also contribute to peer-reviewed journals, often in collaboration with academic supervisors. At the same time, all students will read scientific writing in books and journals as part of their studies, including as research for their own writing.

In contrast, the term 'science writing' is commonly used to refer to less technical writing intended for a general audience. This involves communicating important or interesting information about science and technology in an accessible or entertaining manner, often within a broader social context. This kind of writing may be in the form of books, articles or blogs. Scientists may be involved in this type of writing, but it is often produced by non-scientists, many of whom are journalists with a professional interest in science. There is no obligation for scientists or science students to read this type of writing, and it does not count as a reliable source of evidence for academic work. However, it is often of interest and can help scientists to understand how the general public access and perceive scientific information.

As with most categorisations, there are some fuzzy boundaries. Take, for example, a patent application, which is a legal as well as a technical document. A patent has a complex readership, and this means that the authors are faced with some difficult writing choices, as will be discussed later in this chapter.

3 Analysis of different types of writing in the sciences

In this section, we will analyse a range of texts dealing with science and identify some shared characteristics, as well as some differences. These extracts have been chosen both because they come from reputable sources and because they are relatively comprehensible to people not specialising in the particular discipline from which they come. They still, however, contain specialised vocabulary which you may not know. With this in mind, as you read, focus on understanding the general gist of the text, or just 'getting a feel for it'; don't worry too much about individual words and phrases which are unfamiliar. The object here is to explore different kinds of writing in the sciences, not to study particular disciplines in detail.

■ Explorative Task

Quickly read the texts that follow to get a general idea of their content, and make a few notes on the following questions:

1) What kind of text is it? (essay, report, article, book, blog etc.)

2) What topic or discipline does it represent?

3) Who seems to have written it? (student, academic, professional, journalist etc.)

4) What kind of reader will probably read the text?

5) Is it possible to say something about the writer's purpose in the text as a whole or in this part of the text?

6) What do you think is 'scientific' about the text?

■ **Text A**

Epidemiological evidence indicates that hand-transmission is a major contributing factor in the acquisition and spread of Healthcare Associated Infection (HCAI) (Loveday et al, 2014). For this reason, healthcare workers' hand hygiene is traditionally considered as the single most important factor in the reduction of HCAI (Gould et al, 2017). Studies on the effects of handwashing protocols in healthcare settings date back to the mid 1800s (WHO, 2009), but it was not until 2001 that the first national evidence-based guidelines for preventing HCAI in NHS hospitals, including hand hygiene as one of its principle interventions, were introduced by the Department of Health in the UK (Loveday et al, 2014).

This essay will begin by outlining current handwashing practices in healthcare settings, with particular reference to national NHS guidelines. It will then examine current evidence, including systematic reviews, in order to critically evaluate the extent to which particular practices can reduce HCAI. The main focus will be on the effectiveness of cleaning agents and the issue of compliance. It will conclude with suggestions on recommendations for nursing practice and suggestions regarding which areas can be usefully investigated further.

■ **Text B**

Eye-tracking is a technique for monitoring the point of gaze, or eye movements [1], enabling gaze-control [2-4]. Prior research in this area identifies several challenges for users including 1) Midas touch [5]; 2) target selection [6-8]; 3) creative tasks [9]; and 4) scrolling documents [10,11]. Huang and Westin [12] found that ease of use is associated with eye tracking fidelity and effective user interfaces. There is a great deal of research addressing these issues. However, gaze-control usability among disabled people is less discussed.

■ **Text C**

As part of my Industry Based Learning (IBL) placement, I worked at Experian, contributing to the creation of a new tool for web engagement analytics. I was impressed by the rapport the team had with each other and how welcome and valued I felt for the duration of my project work at the company. I noticed that the software development team had regular contact with a number of potential clients, and this seemed to result in ensuring that the product would satisfy their needs.

■ **Text D**

The use of solar water heaters is rapidly increasing in both homes and businesses, as these heaters provide an environmentally friendly and cost-effective source of energy (Tian and Castillo 2016). However, significant improvement to heating efficiency is required before solar water heaters can be used without a supplementary energy source. Various factors in the design of the water heater affect how well solar energy is converted into heat energy, and how effectively the heat is then transferred to the water. This experiment investigated two factors affecting the heating efficiency of solar water heaters: mass flow rate and collector design. Efficiency of a flat-plate collector was measured, and the effects of different methods of welding water tubes to the absorber plate were compared.

■ **Text E**

An organism may comprise just a single cell (unicellular), a collection of cells that are not morphologically or functionally differentiated (colonial), or several distinct cell types with specialised functions (multicellular). Among microorganisms, all bacteria and protozoans are unicellular; fungi may be unicellular or multicellular, while algae may exist in all three forms. There is, however, one way that organisms can be differentiated from each other that is even more fundamental than whether they are uni- or multicellular. It is a difference that is greater than that between a lion and a mushroom or between an earthworm and an oak tree, and it exists at the level of the individual cell. All organisms are made up of one or other (definitely not both!) of two very distinct cell types, which we call procaryotic and eucaryotic cells*, both of which exist in the microbial world. These differ from each other in many ways, including size, structural complexity and organisation of genetic material (Table 3.1).

*The names given to the two cell types derive from Greek words:
Procaryotic = 'before nucleus' Eucaryotic = 'true nucleus'

■ **Text F**

Coid et al. (2006) estimate that 4 per cent of people in Great Britain have a personality disorder. The British Psychological Society suggests that a higher proportion of the population, 10 per cent, meet the criteria for a personality disorder diagnosis and that prevalence is much higher among psychiatric patients. They highlight some studies which suggest that in excess of 80 per cent of psychiatric outpatients and between 50 per cent and 78 per cent of adult prisoners meet the criteria (Alwin et al., 2006).

The National Institute for Health and Clinical Excellence issued guidelines for the treatment and management of borderline personality disorder (NICE, 2009a). The guidelines represent suicide attempts as a defining feature of the diagnosis, with some studies suggesting that suicide rates can be as high as 10 per cent. The Department of Health (2009b) estimates that 5 per cent of the population have a personality disorder. NICE also highlights the economic impact of personality disorder. Guidelines outline a significant financial cost to the health care system, social services and wider society, and estimate the annual cost to the NHS at approximately £61.2 million, 91 per cent of this accounted for by in-patient care. They also estimate that people with personality disorder cost primary care services alone an average of £3,000 per person per year.

■ **Text G**

Using an age-structured transmission dynamic model, we explored different scenarios for COVID-19 transmission and control in the general population of the UK. We found that moderate interventions lasting for 12 weeks, such as school closures, self-isolation of symptomatic individuals, or shielding of older people, would probably not have been suffi-cient to control the epidemic and to avoid far exceeding available ICU capacity, even when these measures were used in combination. In particular, school closures had little effect in our projections, despite our model accounting for substantial asymptomatic transmission among children.[16] This contrasts with strategies aimed at suppressing the spread of pandemic influ-enza, for which school closures are often a key intervention.[16, 31] However, we estimated that a scenario in which more intense lockdown measures were implemented for shorter periods, against a general background of physical distancing measures, might be able to keep pro-jected case numbers at a level that would not overwhelm the health system. These findings are consistent with studies that explored subsets of these control measures for COVID-19 in the UK,[11] France,[15] the USA,[12] and Canada.[13] However, we integrate model trajectories over a distribution of values for R_0 and seeding dates to provide uncertainty bounds for our pro-jections, explore the impact of alternative timings of interventions, and account for variation in the proportion of symptomatic cases by age as estimated from case data.[16] Directly compar-ing these projections to the ongoing COVID-19 epidemic in the UK is complicated because enacted control measures have not exactly followed the scenarios outlined here. However, as a point of comparison, recent empirical estimates of the reproduction number in the UK[32, 33] are compatible with our assumptions concerning R_0 and the impact of lockdown measures (appendix p 13).

■ Text H

The growth medium in some aspects of the present invention is a liquid growth medium, i.e. any medium that is suitable for microbial growth. In this specification reference, liquid means liquid according to the conventional sense of the word, and would be understood by the skilled person to mean free flowing or capable of being poured. In this context liquid media can also refer to viscous liquids, viscosified to provide easier handling and resistance to spillage from the incubation vessel in such an assay. Such viscosity can result from, for example, the addition of agar or other gelling agents in amounts too low to form conventional plate media. Concentrations of agar less than 0.5% should be effective in the liquid media used in the present invention.

■ Text I

Artificial intelligence and facial analysis software is becoming commonplace in job inter-views. The technology, developed by US company HireVue, analyses the language and tone of a candidate's voice and records their facial expressions as they are videoed answer-ing identical questions.

It was used in the UK for the first time in September but has been used around the world for several years. Some 700 companies, including Vodafone, Hilton and Urban Outfitters have tried it out.

Certainly there are significant benefits to be had from this. HireVue says it speeds up the hiring process by 90% thanks to the speed of information processing. But there are important risks we should be wary of when outsourcing job interviews to AI.

The AI is built on algorithms that assess applicants against its database of about 25,000 pieces of facial and linguistic information. These are compiled from previous interviews of "successful hires" – those who have gone on to be good at the job. The 350 linguistic elements include criteria like a candidate's tone of voice, their use of passive or active words, sentence length and the speed they talk. The thousands of facial features analysed include brow furrowing, brow raising, the amount eyes widen or close, lip tightening, chin raising and smiling.

■ Text J

If, in some cataclysm, all of scientific knowledge were to be destroyed, and only one sentence passed on to the next generations of creatures, what statement would contain the most information in the fewest words? I believe it is the *atomic hypothesis* (or the atomic fact, or whatever you want to call it) *that all things are made of atoms – little particles that move around in perpetual motion, attracting each other when they are a little distance apart, but repelling upon being squeezed into one another.* In that one sentence, you will see, there is an *enormous* amount of information about the world, if just a little imagination and thinking are applied.

■ Text K

It is a daily matter to look around a typical laboratory and note the imbalance of the sexes in different roles. In a lab using animals, there may be a fair number of female technicians, but PI is more likely than not to be a man. In a computer laboratory, women are in short supply at all levels, despite the prevalence of women as 'computers' in the early days of the subject. Read *Programmed Inequality* by Marie Hicks for a stark description of how the roles of women, in what would now be called data science, were systematically downgraded and men were inserted at the top levels, for instance in the UK's Civil Service in the 1950's and 60's.

TEXT DETAILS

Text A (Bottomley and Pryjmachuk, 2017: 51–52) is a model example of an undergraduate student's **essay** on handwashing in healthcare settings. It is the 'Introduction' section.

Text B (Huang and Westin, 2020) is from a Master's student's **research report** on technology used to aid people with disabilities. It is a section entitled 'Related work', following the introduction.

Text C is a piece of **reflective writing** from the Monash University website. It forms part of a series of activities to help science students improve their skills in this area.

Text D is also from the Monash University website, and is an example of a student **lab report**.

Text E (Hogg, 2005: 51) is from a widely used microbiology **textbook** aimed at introducing students to the subject. This extract discusses cells in organisms. It is written by an academic.

Text F (Castillo, 2013: 18) is from a **book** on mental health and psychiatric practice, written for students and professionals in various areas of practice. This extract is from a section on personality disorders. It is written by an academic.

Text G (Davies et al.: 382) is from the discussion section of a **journal article** related to COVID-19 in the highly regarded medical journal, *The Lancet*. It is written by academics.

Text H (Turner and Burton, 2018) is an extract from a **patent** (a document applying for the legal right to make or sell an invention for a period of 20 years from the date of the application). This particular patent was written by the inventors themselves, chemists working in industry, under legal guidance.

Text I (Manhoka, 2019) is an **article** from *The Conversation*, an online journal in which academics aim to present their work to the public, and other academics, in an accessible way. This forum is a relatively new initiative which reflects the growing awareness in universities of the need to communicate ideas beyond the world of academia.

Text J is from a **book** on physics by the famous physicist Richard Feynman (2011: 4). It is one of those rare books which have managed to reach out beyond the world of academia and capture the public imagination. There are a number of scientists who have managed to do this, including Stephen Hawking, with his book, *A brief history of time* (1998).

Text K (Donald, 2020) is from a popular **blog** called *Occam's Typewriter*, which brings together many academics who like to blog about science and other topics. (The name is a play on the term 'Occam's Razor', usually explained as the concept that the simplest explanation is usually right.) The piece is written by Athene Donald, a Cambridge University physicist with an interest in gender issues.

4 Text features

The texts are characterised by having a particular <u>purpose</u> related to **the communication of scientific knowledge**. Each text is written for a designated <u>audience</u>, a reader who is interested in this knowledge, and the source of the text can tell us about this audience. This may be an academic audience in the same field, an academic audience outside the field, a general non-academic audience, a professional audience or some combination of these. The texts contain different degrees of <u>technical language</u>, i.e. discipline-specific language, depending on the purpose of the text and its audience.

Table 1.1 provides a summary of these characteristics, along with details and examples:

Table 1.1

Topic	Purpose	Audience	Technical Language
A Hand-washing in healthcare settings	To introduce an essay and outline the structure of the essay	A lecturer in the same field who will assess the work	Epidemiological, infection, HCAI, NHS, interventions
B Eye-movement technology	To explain previous research on the topic of the report and identify a research gap	A lecturer in the same field who will assess the work; researchers	Eye-tracking, gaze-control, interface
C Work placement	To reflect on an experience	A lecturer in the same field who will assess the work	Web engagement analytics, software
D Solar water heaters	To introduce the background to an experiment	A lecturer in the same field who will assess the work	Solar, mass flow rate, flat-plate collector
E Cells in organisms	To introduce and explain the chapter topic, including key terms and definitions	A student beginning their university studies in biology/microbiology	Organism, cell, morphologically, microorganisms, prokaryotic, eucaryotic, nucleus, bacteria, protozoans, unicellular, multicellular, fungi, algae, microbial, genetic material
F Personality disorders	To present background information on the chapter topic, including statistics and guidelines	Mental health professionals and students	Personality disorder, The British Psychological Society, diagnosis, patients, NICE, NHS
G COVID-19	To discuss the findings of a study	Researchers in the same field	Transmission, COVID-19, interventions, self-isolation, symptomatic, shielding, epidemic, ICU, asymptomatic, pandemic, influenza, lockdown, physical distancing, control measures

Topic	Purpose	Audience	Technical Language
H Growth media for detection of microbes	To introduce and define some key terminology necessary for a patent application for an invention	Specialist companies and researchers working in the same field; legal entities	Growth medium, microbial, viscous, viscosified, incubation, vessel, assay, viscosity, agar, gelling agent, plate media
I AI	To introduce an aspect of AI technology	Other academics and the general public	Artificial intelligence, AI, facial analysis software, information processing, algorithms, linguistic
J Scientific knowledge	To introduce the concept of scientific knowledge	The general public	Atomic hypothesis, atoms, particles, perpetual motion
K Gender in science	To introduce the issue of gender in science	Other academics and the general public	PI, data science

5 Text types

Texts A-H are examples of what we have termed 'scientific writing', i.e. texts written by scientists for other scientists. Texts A-D are academic texts exemplifying some of the assignment types that science students may need to complete at university. Texts E-H represent writing by academics which is at the same time typical reading for students and researchers: books, textbooks and journal articles. These scientific writing texts follow academic conventions such as making reference to sources. Texts I, J and K are examples of what we have previously defined as 'science writing', and they might also be termed 'popular science'. They comprise attempts by academics (in these cases) to communicate scientific knowledge to a relatively general, or non-expert audience. But even these three texts represent quite distinct forms of communication. The article in *The Conversation* is mainly plain in style, focussing on conveying information in a clear, accessible way. The blog is a more conversational and narrative account. Richard Feynman uses a playful tone in his book, informing and entertaining, reaching out to his non-expert audience in a way that he clearly hopes will reassure them that physics needn't be too scary!

6 Audience and purpose

We can discuss the purpose of a text as a whole, or the purpose of a particular part of a text. We might also use words like 'aim', 'goal' and 'function'. These ideas will be important when we come to discuss your own writing. In writing, the audience is your reader. Audience is also a concept which will be discussed in detail in this book with reference to your own writing. Audience and purpose will determine the choices you make in terms of content, organisation and language, among other things. Many official bodies representing scientists stress the need to be able to communicate clearly with different audiences. The Royal Society of Chemistry, for example, stresses the need for chemists to adapt what they say for "audiences of different abilities and knowledge".

Patents can tell us a lot about some of the complexities of audience and purpose. This type of text could be written by scientists working in industry and medicine, or by researchers in universities. Michael Burton, co-author of the patent quoted earlier in the chapter, discusses the purpose of patents and the different audiences that a patent writer has to consider, together with how these affect choices the writer makes. You will look at an excerpt from this discussion in the Reflective Task that follows.

■ Reflective Task

Read the interview excerpt and note the different audiences that the interviewee mentions, and the different choices writers have to make to meet the needs and expectations of those audiences.

In short, patents are a marketing tool with two audiences: customers – to draw them in; competitors – to keep them out. And although their purpose is essentially commercial, patents are supposed to be accurate and do make a substantial contribution to the scientific literature. Before a patent can be granted, the patent application must go through a review process, the 'examination', which can be very vigorous, with the examiner. Although the examiner probably has a scientific background, they are not necessarily an expert or someone with in-depth knowledge of the field, as would be the case with normal peer review. Refreshingly, in the world of patents, it is assumed that the inventor *is* an expert in the field and he or she is, therefore, given more scope in certain matters relating to the drafting of the patent specification. As an example, inventors are allowed to choose and define their own nomenclature – within obvious limits – without the constraints applied during a standard peer review. On the other hand, some of the legal wording has to be very precise, and correspond to well-established legal language and precedents, so the document can be a strange hybrid. Ultimately, commercial considerations are the main drivers for obtaining patent protection, and the protection is defined by the claims, hence the importance of a good patent lawyer.

(Burton, 2020)

7 Language

■ Technical language

You will notice that technical, or discipline-specific, terminology used in the articles covers a wide range of language: some terms, like 'prokaryotic', are highly technical and, without accompanying definitions, would only be understood by people familiar with the field;

others, like 'diagnosis', are accessible to non-experts. Terms like 'COVID-19', 'shielding' and 'self-isolation' have become a fairly commonplace part of public discourse because of the particular circumstances of 2020, which serves to demonstrate the sometimes fluid nature of scientific knowledge and language. Choosing the right technical language for your purpose and audience will be an important part of the writing you do at university.

■ Academic language

Academic texts are often characterised by not only the high percentage of technical words which they contain, but also by the high percentage of 'academic' language that they contain. A useful resource with regard to this is the *Academic Word List*, developed by Averil Coxhead at the University of Wellington in New Zealand. This is a list of the most common words in academia (discounting technical terms and common everyday words). The extracts from academic texts analysed in this chapter contain a high number of these words, including 'analyse', 'evidence', 'protocols', 'factors' and 'impact'; the less academic texts contain fewer of these words.

■ Informal language

In contrast to the academic texts, the three popular science texts contain some rather informal expression which is less common in an academic context, e.g. 'try something out', 'speed something up', 'little particles', 'just a little', 'whatever you wish to call it', 'a fair number of' and 'more likely than not'. We might also note the use in these informal texts of short paragraphs, imperative verb forms and rhetorical questions; academic texts are much less likely to contain these features.

■ Reflective language

Text C, the reflection, is slightly different from the examples of other types of written assignment in terms of language. Reflective writing differs in tone from other types of academic writing. It requires you to consider your experiences and feelings, and the style of writing is therefore rather personal. This is reflected in the use of personal pronouns, and a narrative style.

> As part of **my** Industry Based Learning (IBL) placement, **I worked** at Experian, contributing to the creation of a new tool for web engagement analytics. **I was impressed** by the rapport the team had with each other and how welcome and valued **I felt** for the duration of **my** project work at the company. **I noticed** that the software development team had regular contact with a number of potential clients, and this seemed to result in ensuring that the product would satisfy their needs.

Some journal reflections may be quite informal. Essay reflections, on the other hand, often retain elements of academic style, as illustrated by Text C ('contributing to', 'for the duration of', 'this seemed to result in ensuring', 'satisfy their needs').

Note that the use of personal pronouns is not restricted to reflective writing. For example, Text G uses the pronoun 'we' to report the research process. This will be discussed more in Chapter 3.

8 Popular science

Your focus while at university will be on reading the textbooks and journal articles which will help you succeed in your assignments. However, it is also useful for your broader development as a scientist to follow how your discipline and other scientific disciplines are reported to the general public. One popular semi-academic scientific publication is *The New Scientist*. In June 2020, it featured articles on the following:

- COVID-19
- In vitro fertilisation (IVF)
- Artificial intelligence (AI) and Disney
- Military weapons
- Astronomy
- Fires in the Amazon and the Arctic
- The link between Black Lives Matter and the environment

It is clear that topics cover a wide range, from AI to IVF, from astronomy to infectious diseases. Furthermore, it is clear that this publication places science in a clear social context, with links to public health, the environment, politics and even entertainment.

■ Explorative Task

1) Go to The New Scientist or Scientific American websites or look at a similar publication. (Many university libraries will have subscriptions to these publications.)

2) Scan the homepage and type key words into the search facility to find any articles related to your discipline.

3) Have a look at these articles. What do you think about the way that they approach and explain the facts and the issues? What social context is provided?

The following reflective and review tasks will help you to consolidate your understanding of Chapter 1.

■ Reflective Task

1) What kind of writing in science do you read regularly?

2) What kind of scientific texts do you have experience writing?

3) Which of these do you most enjoy or feel comfortable writing?

4) What are the main challenges for you when reading or writing scientific texts?

■ Review Task

1) Select a text that you have written or are in the process of writing.

2) Try to improve the text by focusing on purpose, audience and language.

> In this chapter, we have looked at writing in the sciences from your perspective as a reader. In the next chapter, we will apply some of the concepts discussed here to your own writing.

Sources of example texts

Bottomley, J. and Pryjmachuk, S. (2017) *Critical thinking skills for your nursing degree*. St Albans: Critical Publishing.

Castillo, H. (2013) Service-user insights into recovery in personality disorder. In S. Walker (ed) *Modern mental health: Critical perspectives on psychiatric practice*. St Albans: Critical Publishing.

Davies, N. G., Kucharski, A. J., Eggo, R. M., Gimma, A. and Edmunds, W. J. (2020) Effects of non-pharmaceutical interventions on COVID-19 cases, deaths, and demand for hospital services in the UK: A modelling study. *The Lancet*, 5, 375–385.

Donald, A. (2020) *Sex, gender, research and fairness*. Available at: http://occamstypewriter. org/athenedonald/ (accessed 14th December, 2020).

Feynman, R. (2011) *Six easy pieces: The fundamentals of science explained*. London: Penguin.

Hogg, S. (2005) *Essential microbiology*. New York: John Wiley & Sons Ltd.

Huang, L. and Westin, T. (2020) Evaluating challenges of unimodal gaze-control for motor disabled people. *International Conference on Human-Computer Interaction (HCI)*.

Manokha, I. (2019) Facial analysis AI is being used in job interviews – it will probably reinforce inequality. In *The Conversation*, 7th October. Available at: https://theconversation. com/facial-analysis-ai-is-being-used-in-job-interviews-it-will-probably-reinforce-in-equality-124790 (accessed 30th June, 2020).

Monash University. *Reflective writing in IT.* Available at: www.monash.edu/rlo/assignment-samples/information-technology/reflective-writing-in-it (accessed 10th January, 2021).

Monash University. *Writing a science lab report.* Available at: www.monash.edu/rlo/assignment-samples/science/science-writing-a-lab-report (accessed 30th June, 2020).

Turner, H. J. and Burton, M. (2018) US Patent for Naphthalene derived chromogenic enzyme substrates. Patent # 10,443,084. *USPTO.* Available at: http://patft.uspto.gov/netacgi/nph-Parser?Sect1=PTO2&Sect2=HITOFF&p=1&u=%2Fnetahtml%2FPTO%2Fsearch-bool.html&r=1&f=G&l=50&col=AND&d=PTXT&s1=10443084.PN.&OS=PN/10443084&RS=PN/10443084 (accessed 27th December, 2020).

References

Academic Word List. Available at: www.wgtn.ac.nz/lals/resources/academicwordlist (accessed 11th December, 2020).

Burton, Michael (2020) *Reflections on patent writing.* Email correspondence with Jane Bottomley, 20th January 2020.

Feliú-Mójer, M. I. (2015) Effective communication, better science. In *Scientific American*, 24th February. Available at: https://blogs.scientificamerican.com/guest-blog/effective-communication-better-science/ (accessed 15th December, 2020).

Gullers, A. (2020) Experts will propose communication in education. In *EECS Internal News, KTH*, 9th December. Available at: https://intra.kth.se/en/eecs/aktuellt-pa-eecs/nyheter/mer-kommunikation-i-forskarutbildningen-1.1034747 (accessed 10th December, 2020).

Hawkin, S. (1998) *A brief history of time* (10th edition). New York: Bantam Books.

Hofmann, A. H. (2019) *Scientific writing and communication: Papers, proposals and presentations* (4th edition). Oxford: Oxford University Press.

New Scientist. Available at: www.newscientist.com/ (accessed 24th June, 2020).

Royal Society of Chemistry. *Employability skills.* Available at: https://edu.rsc.org/future-in-chemistry/career-options/employability-skills (accessed 3rd January, 2021).

Scientific American. Available at: https://blogs.scientificamerican.com/guest-blog/effective-communication-better-science/ (accessed 15th December, 2020).

CHAPTER 2

Writing at university

This chapter will discuss what it means to write at university, and how you can develop as a writer during your studies, and beyond, in your professional life. It will guide you through the writing process, and help you to understand how to fully engage with it in order to complete assignments to the very best of your ability. It will examine the different stages of this process, including analysing the task, researching the topic, and selecting, evaluating and organising information and ideas. It will explain the importance of drafting and editing, and look at issues around formatting and proofreading. It will explore some general principles which can be applied to different types of scientific writing.

1 Writing as a university student

As a science student, you need to assimilate a great deal of information, and engage in new ideas and intellectual processes. Moreover, you need to develop a range of academic skills, including communication skills. This includes developing proficiency in scientific writing and learning how to produce the different types of written text required as part of your studies.

1.1 A community of writers

Every student writing at university is part of what is sometimes called a 'discourse community', a group of students, researchers and academics who share ways of thinking about, discussing and reporting on a particular area of study. These groups have certain knowledge, values and practices in common. This helps determine the kind of discourse, i.e. written and spoken texts, that characterises their discipline. For anyone working or studying within a particular discourse community, it is important to understand how the people in that community communicate, and what text types, language and conventions they use to do this. It is also important to understand

DOI: 10.4324/9781003118572-3

that most members of a discourse community, whatever stage they are at in their studies or careers, sometimes struggle with writing, and look for ways to improve their knowledge and skills in this area. They all need to develop systematic approaches to writing and evolve a range of strategies that will help them take a piece of writing from its beginnings to its final form. Elements of this approach will differ according to individual preferences and ways of working, but there are some fairly general principles which can also inform this process. The writing process will be discussed in the next section, but before that, take some time to reflect on where you are now as a writer.

■ Reflective Task

Consider the following questions.

1) Do you enjoy writing? Why? Why not?

2) What types of writing have you done in the past?

3) What language or languages do you have most experience of writing in?

4) How do you usually approach a writing task?

5) What kind of comments have teachers or other students made on your writing in the past?

6) How do you tend to respond to feedback you receive on your writing?

Students using this book will have different feelings and experiences about writing, some positive and some negative. It is important to reflect on these feelings and experiences and to think about how best to go forward from this point. This involves identifying strengths and weaknesses, as well as exploring strategies for improvement. The strategies you adopt can impact on your university studies and beyond, in your professional life. The aim is not perfection; it is rather a case of making many small improvements over time, recognising successful strategies and outcomes, and sometimes persevering in the face of disappointment or obstacles. I have personally seen many students make great strides in their writing, sometimes after a shaky start. What these students have in common is a positive attitude, an ability to reflect on and critically assess their own work, and a willingness to seek and act on advice.

1.2 Typical writing assignments at university
The type of writing assignment that you are required to write at university will depend on your discipline. However, the following are common in most scientific subjects:

- Essays
- Research reports
- Lab reports
- Reviews of articles or other types of literature

- Reviews of the literature on a topic
- Reflective accounts
- Dissertations

Written assignments will relate directly to the learning outcomes of a particular module, and they will be assessed with reference to assessment guidelines and assessment criteria, which in turn relate to the learning outcomes. This alignment is designed to ensure that there is clarity and transparency regarding how students' performance and progress is measured.

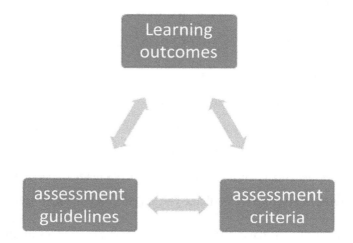

Figure 2.1 Assessment

It is therefore very important that you familiarise yourself with all the course documentation as part of the writing process. This will be discussed in more detail later in the chapter.

1.3 Responding to feedback on your writing

One of the most important roles that lecturers perform is to give feedback to students on the work they produce. This can be 'formative', i.e. advice on how to improve their work in future tasks, or it can be 'summative', i.e. feedback on an assessed piece of work to explain why a particular mark has been awarded; the latter tells a student how they have met, or failed to meet, the marking criteria attached to the task.

It is crucial to your studies that you know how to access, understand and respond to feedback. No matter what mark you receive for an assignment, it is very important to know in what ways you did well or didn't do well and to know how to respond in a constructive manner.

Some common writing issues which emerge in feedback are:

- **A lack of coherence**: This usually means ideas and arguments are hard to follow because they do not make sense or flow easily. This may be because the way things have been organised is confusing, or some information may be missing or irrelevant. It may be because ideas are not linked together in a clear way. These issues will be further discussed in Chapter 6 and in Chapter 8.

- **A lack of criticality**: This usually means it isn't clear that the writer is saying something meaningful about the topic based on what they believe to be true having done the research. This often manifests itself in uncritical use of sources, leading to a 'patchwork' of descriptions of the literature, rather than the writer's own analysis, interpretation, evaluation and synthesis of the arguments and evidence. This will be further discussed in Chapter 7 and Chapter 8.
- **Issues with style**. This may mean that the language is too informal, that the tone is too conversational or 'chatty'. Or it may be that the language is somewhat 'strange'. This unusual language may be language that is found in a thesaurus, language that is perhaps anachronistic or rather literary. As we will see in Chapter 3, scientific style is often largely neutral in style, albeit with important use of technical and academic language.
- **Issues with grammatical accuracy**. This usually means that there are too many basic errors. The most important thing is that writing is understandable and easy to read, and a few minor grammatical mistakes should not be an issue. However, too many basic errors make a text look unprofessional, and the assessor may feel that the writer has demonstrated insufficient care and a failure to proofread. Comments on grammar can also refer to more serious problems with syntax and cohesion, and these can seriously hinder communication. Chapter 4 and Chapter 5 include information on how to construct clear, grammatically accurate sentences; Chapter 6 deals with cohesion, i.e. grammar beyond the sentence; Appendix 1 and Appendix 2 provide additional grammatical information on noun and verb phrases; Appendix 3 highlights some common language difficulties.
- **Issues with referencing**. This may be because the writer has not followed accepted conventions on referencing, as presented in a particular style guide, or has failed to follow local guidelines they have been given. This will be further discussed in Chapter 9.

1.4 Finding support

If you find you need help with your writing, you are likely to find a range of support at your university. This may take the form of online resources, classes, workshops or individual consultations. The latter involves meeting with an expert in English language and academic skills to discuss a piece of your writing. This could be an assignment for which you have already received a mark and feedback, or an assignment which you are currently working on. In the former case, the tutor will be able to help you understand why you received the mark and the feedback you did. In the latter case, the tutor will be able to help you improve the piece of work before submission. In both cases, the real focus should be less on that particular piece of work, and more on you as a developing academic writer. The tutor may help you to correct some errors of grammar and punctuation, but they are quite likely to focus on wider issues of clarity, coherence, style and readability. They will often act as a 'critical friend', asking you to articulate your argument, or giving you a sense of the reader's experience as they move through the text. This process, along with any direct advice you receive, should help you develop your academic writing skills and apply these to future work.

1.5 Being a happier writer . . . ☺

In my experience as a teacher, students can often struggle to write clearly and meaningfully because they are somewhat daunted by or detached from the process. They may feel it is purely something that they have to get done in order to complete an assignment and fulfil an obligation. Writing like this can be a miserable experience! If you can approach writing in another way, treating it as an opportunity to say something interesting about what you know and believe, and giving yourself time and space to experiment with conveying this message, then it can become a much more pleasurable experience. We will talk more about reading and editing your own text in section 2, but for now, think about reading what you've written, not just to find errors or problems, but to find parts that seem to work well. Imagine someone reading these parts and being impressed with your work!

2 The writing process

Many scientists enjoy writing. However, over the years, a fair number of my science students have told me that they have a tendency to put off writing, sometimes till the very last minute. This is often because they view writing as rather daunting, or sometimes just uninteresting. Added to this, these students are often absorbed by the research process itself, in particular, the exciting work they are doing in the lab or in the field. To be excited about these is a good thing of course, but this really shouldn't come at the expense of writing. As we discussed in Chapter 1, communication skills are widely considered to be as important as technical skills in the world of science, and the good work students do in the lab or the field or the library will be wasted if they do not successfully convey their new knowledge and understanding through the texts they produce for assignments. The fact is that it takes most people a lot of time and effort to produce a text which is clear, readable and professional. It requires a careful, systematic approach covering a number of stages.

2.1 The different stages of the writing process

Each stage of the writing process contributes to the final product, and the work you do as part of this process will determine the quality and readability of the text you produce. These stages generally include:

- Analysing the assignment
- Researching the topic
- Selecting, evaluating and organising information
- Drafting and editing your text
- Compiling a list of references
- Formatting your text
- Proofreading your text

However, the process is not linear: elements of it are interchangeable, overlapping or cyclical.

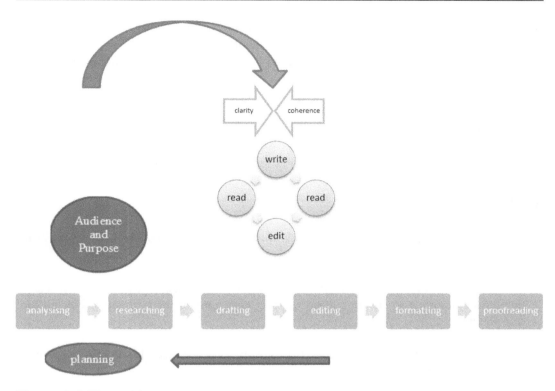

Figure 2.2 The writing process

The discussion in this section will now centre on the type of writing assignment that requires you to demonstrate your knowledge and understanding of a particular area of science with reference to the literature. This is a common type of assignment at most levels of taught university study in the sciences, and it is one which is reflected in the literature reviews which form part of the introduction in typical IMRAD research reports (▶**Chapter 8**). Moreover, much of the discussion here, on planning or editing for example, can be generalised to other types of scientific writing.

2.2 Analysing the assignment

In Chapter 1, we saw that texts are defined primarily by their audience and purpose, and this is also the starting point for your own writing. It is your audience and purpose which will determine how you approach the assignment. Swales and Feak put this very nicely in their book *Academic writing for graduate students*:

Audience, purpose, and strategy are typically interconnected. If the audience knows less than the writer, the writer's purpose is often instructional (as in a textbook). If the audience knows more than the writer, the writer's purpose is usually to *display* familiarity, expertise, and intelligence.

(Swales and Feak, 2012: 10)

When writing assignments at university, you are in Swales and Feak's second category, and so your goal is to display your knowledge and understanding to the best of your ability.

In order to refine your purpose, it is necessary to look closely at the assignment task, to analyse it, or 'unpack' it, and break it down into its constituent parts. One strategy can be to underline key words and try to identify:

- The general topic
- The focus of the assignment
- Instruction or command words which indicate what you need to do

■ Practice Task (i)

Look at the following writing assignment tasks and identify the general topic, the focus of the assignment and any instruction words.

> Many medical devices are fitted with different kinds of alarms. Discuss how these alarms should be designed to ensure a good working environment for staff and safe healthcare for patients.

> Outline the current plastic pollution challenge and propose possible solutions with reference to green chemistry.

It is important to differentiate between different instruction words and to understand their precise meanings, as these determine, for example, the scope and depth of the work required, or the level of criticality you will need to apply. It is one thing to 'describe' a system and another to 'analyse' or 'evaluate' it; it is yet another thing to 'compare and contrast' different systems. Likewise, 'explaining' a framework is very different from 'applying' it, though you might be asked to do both of course. There are many resources which list these instruction verbs – though they may call them different things – alongside their definitions, including many university websites, for example:

- Massey University (Command words)
- Monash University (Assignment direction words)

You may wish to consult these sources to complete the following Practice Task. You may also find learner's dictionaries to be useful, for example the online Cambridge Dictionary.

■ Practice Task (ii)

Match the instruction words in bold with their definitions.

1 **Describe** and explain the working principle behind typical robot sensors . . .	a Look at something in detail by breaking it down into its constituent parts
2 Describe and **explain** the working principle behind typical robot sensors . . .	b Describe the main features of something
3 **Outline** the causes of air pollution . . .	c Discuss similarities and differences between things
4 **Define** the term 'ecosystem' . . .	d Use something for a practical purpose
5 **Analyse** the impact of globalisation on . . .	e Present a topic in detail considering different angles and opinions
6 . . . then **evaluate** the public health implications of this intervention . . .	f Make a judgement about something
7 **Compare and contrast** fission and fusion . . .	g Establish what something means
8 . . . then **apply** the adapted framework to the dataset . . .	h Give reasons for something
9 **Discuss** the environmental benefits of carbon capture . . .	i Say what something is like

Not all assignment tasks will contain instruction words. Some may provide a title such as 'Potential green chemistry solutions to the plastic pollution challenge', with guidelines providing more detailed information on what is expected. On some modules, you may be required to formulate your own title related to a particular topic area. In all cases, a close reading of the assessment guidelines and assessment criteria is key to meeting the task requirements. As previously mentioned, these relate directly to the learning outcomes of a course module. The assessment criteria should give you a clear idea of what is expected of you when you complete an assignment. In writing, these will often relate to:

- the quality and relevance of the content you have included, indicating how widely you have read and how well you have understood the topic and the assignment
- the organisation of the content
- the coherence of the ideas and arguments you put forward
- the style, accuracy and precision of your language

Use the assessment criteria of an assignment task as a checklist when making final revisions to your work.

When you are sure about what the assignment task requires of you, it is perhaps time to think about what you already know about the topic from lectures and previous study. You may begin to consider possible responses to the assignment and potential arguments you could make, together with what information you would need to include in each case. However, your ultimate response will emerge out of the next stage of the process: the research.

2.3 Researching the topic

Researching the topic of an assignment involves locating and selecting information which will help you respond effectively. You might start with your lecture notes and the reading list for the module, before looking at the wider literature on the topic. When searching the literature, it is important to consider the status of sources, i.e. which ones are considered to be trustworthy in the academic world. Peer-reviewed journal articles are the most trusted medium for reporting and sharing scientific research. The reviewers are academics in the same field. The most trusted journals are those which have the most rigorous selection and editing process. It is important to know which journals are respected in your discipline or field, as some journals may not meet sufficiently high standards to be considered as credible sources. The popular science articles we looked at in Chapter 1 may be written by respected academics and journalists and published in reputable publications, but they are not subject to the same level of scrutiny as peer-reviewed journal articles and so are not considered as suitable academic sources. Even books and conference proceedings, though often viable sources, are less rigorous in their procedures than respected peer-reviewed journals.

Finding potential sources involves using your university library's search facilities. Searches need to be conducted skilfully and search results need to be handled with care. It is important that you use strategies to either narrow or widen your search when appropriate. Ultimately, you are likely to end up with a huge amount of material to look through so it is important that you devise strategies for selecting the most relevant. Use titles, abstracts, introductions, conclusions and headings to find material which relates directly to your writing purpose.

2.4 Selecting, evaluating and organising information and ideas

As you take notes, try to identify the **themes** which emerge in relation to the topic and focus of the assignment. Use your notes to organise and relate information. Think about how what you find out supports or challenges possible responses to the assignment task. Consider too signs of consensus or disagreement in the literature. Identify arguments and examine their strengths and weaknesses. Assess the evidence critically. Reflect on how arguments and evidence in the literature might support or challenge your own emerging position.

Use your notes, with their themes and connections, to construct a basic outline for your writing, with possible headings and subheadings, and links to relevant supporting literature. This is the skeleton of your argument or thread of reasoning. This is what you have decided that you want to say on the topic as a result of your research. It is what you now believe to be true given the evidence that you have been able to find. This is going to make your response original, something that only you can say as it is based on your personal assessment of the literature. You should also record what you *haven't* found out or resolved. These gaps, inconsistencies and doubts are also interesting, and they can form part of a valid response.

Your outline should remain in a fairly fluid state, as when you start writing and developing your ideas, you may well want to revisit and make changes–add things, delete things, move things around. This reflects the fact that the writing process is also part of the thinking process, as will be discussed in the next section.

1) Think carefully about the assignment deadline and the word limit, as this will impact on the work you can do and the scope of your response.

2) As well as adding to your plan, consider if you may need to cut something because it is redundant, irrelevant or takes you above the word limit. You must be selective about what to include. Do not include something just because you have read about it or done a lot of work on it. It is to be expected that some reading will turn out to be irrelevant or insufficiently important, or that it will simply inform your thinking on a topic without needing to be referred to directly.

3) When you add/remove something or reorganise, reassess that the overall coherence of your response or argument has not been disrupted.

2.5 Drafting and editing your text
When writing, many people find a circular approach productive, stopping frequently to read and edit text:

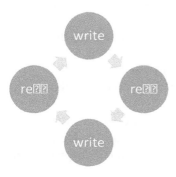

Figure 2.3 The writing cycle

There are two reasons why this approach can benefit you as a writer. Firstly, it can help you clarify your own understanding of the topic and associated ideas and concepts. It is a way of testing your ideas and understanding. As Peter Woodford, a scientist writing about writing, stated long ago in his article *Sounder thinking through clearer writing* (1967: 744): "the very act of writing can help to clarify thinking". Secondly, this approach encourages you to stand back from the page and put yourself in the reader's shoes. It allows you to imagine someone else's experience as they move through the text. It enables you to see if the text is coherent: if it hangs together and makes sense; if it's possible to clearly identify your thread of reasoning, your argument. It helps you ensure that the text is clear and easy to read.

> Peter Woodford writes: "Put down woolly thoughts on paper and their woolliness is immediately exposed." (1967: 744) This is a nice way to put it. 'Woolly' is an informal word which describes either a thick, soft pullover, or ideas which are unclear or confused. Lecturers encountering 'woolly' writing are likely to talk about writing which is 'vague' or which needs to be more 'explicit' when they give feedback. This is a common criticism of student writing at university. Lecturers, like any readers, do not want to have to guess your meaning or work out what you want to say. So this is something to be aware of when you are editing.

When I read students' work, I sometimes find myself asking particular questions. When I have to ask these questions, I wonder if the writer has perhaps not tested their own ideas or considered the reader's experience sufficiently. Here are some of the questions I ask:

- "How does this point relate to the assignment task?"
- "What is the main topic of this section or paragraph and how does it relate to the assignment task?"
- "Why are you saying this *here*, at this point in the text?"
- "What *exactly* do you want to say here?"
- "What does 'it' or 'they' refer to here?"
- "Where are *you* in all this? What do *you* think about this?"

It is worth compiling your own list of questions to use as a reminder when you are editing your work. The Study Box that follows may provide some ideas. The issues that some of these questions raise will be explored in subsequent chapters of the book.

STUDY BOX: WRITING CHECKLIST

1) Is everything in the text relevant to the assignment?

2) Am I making myself clear about what I think about the topic given the research I have done?

3) Is it clear what the main topic of each section and paragraph is and how this relates to the main topic?

4) Is it obvious why something is included in a particular place in the text?

5) Have I made points clearly and explicitly, or am I asking the reader to guess things or work things out? Is anything vague, ambiguous or open to misunderstanding?

6) Is each idea sustained and developed to its conclusion?

7) Would somebody else be able to read this easily and understand what I want to say?

8) Are my sentences easy to follow? Could longer sentences be broken down into shorter ones?

9) Have I used words carefully and precisely?

10) When I write words like 'it', 'they', 'them', 'this', and 'these', is it clear what I am referring to?

■ Explorative Task

These texts were written by a pre-sessional student at the University of Manchester. The student has used the write-read-write approach to redraft their text.

1) Read the two drafts of the text that follow and decide which is clearer and easier to read. Identify the changes that the students has made in order to improve the text.

■ Text A

The Third Generation Partnership Project (3GPP) defined two parts of 3G evolution standards: High Speed Packet Access (HSPA) and Long Term Evolution (LTE) [1]. Both HSPA and LTE have advantages and disadvantages. There are many factors affecting the decision of operators to choose the appropriate evolution standard, such cost and performance [1]. This will be likely to influence operator's decision on network architecture.

In this essay, an overview of 3G technology is outlined. Following this, the merits and demerits of each evolution standard are discussed and some advices are given.

■ Text B

In order to enable existing mobile systems to meet the requirements of modern high-tech development, two 3G evolution standards, as defined by the Third Generation Partnership Project (3GPP), have been proposed: High Speed Packet Access (HSPA) and Long Term Evolution (LTE) [1]. Operators must decide on the most suitable evolution standard for their network; there are a number of factors which will influence this decision, such as cost and performance [1]. Both HSPA and LTE have advantages and disadvantages, as has been documented in the literature [1]. The purpose of this essay is to examine the merits and demerits of HSPA and LTE. The first section provides an overview of 3G technology. This is followed by a discussion of the recent research into the differences between the two evolution standards, along with some recommendations for future practice in the industry.

2) Use your analysis of the text to complete the following paragraph with these words:

   outline; errors; situation; logical; mobile systems

> Text B begins with a clear contextualisation of the current 1) _____ and
> clearly identifies developments in the field of 2) _____. It introduces ideas in
> a 3) _____, step-by-step fashion. It has a clearer 4) _____ of what is to
> follow in the rest of the essay. It has fewer grammatical 5) _____ and more
> natural expression.

1) Do not underestimate how much you will need to read and edit as you write. Some research suggests that writers do this more as they become more experienced writers, not less!

2) Reading aloud can be a useful strategy – it can help you decide if something sounds natural and flows easily from point to point.

3) When asking yourself if you have demonstrated a good understanding of the science, ask yourself if you need to go back to the literature, or discuss the ideas with someone.

4) If you find you are over the word count, be wary of removing individual words or phrases as you can easily destroy the cohesion and coherence of a text like this. It is much better to look at the content as a whole and consider if you can delete, for instance, a particular example.

2.6 Compiling a list of references

You can of course compile your reference list when you've finished everything else, but this is probably a rather inefficient way to do it. Instead, try to keep track of references from the start, using referencing software like Mendeley or Zotero if it helps you.

We will look at referencing conventions in Chapter 9. In Chapter 7, we will focus on active, critical and purposeful use of sources.

2.7 Formatting your text

Formatting is an important element of a text. If you consider it from the point of view of the reader, it can greatly enhance clarity, coherence and readability. Clear, consistent headings and subheadings, consistent spacing, and good use of font and white space help the reader to move quickly and easily through the text. The ideal situation is that they won't even notice the formatting as it does not interfere with their journey through the text. Poor, inconsistent formatting may distract them or cause confusion regarding how things are organised.

2.8 Proofreading your text

Be sure not to confuse editing and proofreading. Editing involves changing content, organisation of information and expression as you process knowledge and refine ideas; this is the process through which you improve clarity and coherence. Proofreading is surface-level checking of grammar and punctuation. This can be done to some degree whilst writing, but there should always be detailed proofreading of the final text when you are fairly sure you do not want to make further substantial changes to content and organisation.

■ Practice Task

Correct the mistakes in grammar and punctuation in the text.

Most universities has Virtual Learning Environments (VLEs) such as blackboard and moodle. It provide online space for course modules where students can access informations on course content, assessment, further study. VLE are also used for the electronic submission of assessed work, that enables lecturers to use software such as turnitin to check for plagiarism in student's work. A further function of VLEs is to provide a space for students enter into discussion with each other. Whilst this would appear to be an excellent opportunity for all students to develop their idea and understanding, and for non-native speakers to practice their language skills, it would seem that many are reluctant to engage in this type of activity, the reasons of this remain unclear.

▶ **Model Text 1, Appendix 4**
▶ **Chapter 4** sentence structure and sentence boundaries
▶ **Chapter 4** relative clauses
▶ **Chapter 5** punctuation
▶ **Chapter 9** spelling
▶ **Appendix 2** noun phrases and articles
▶ **Appendix 3** common errors

Many people ask someone to 'check' their writing, or employ a professional proofreader to do this. There is nothing wrong with this in principle, but be aware that this should ideally take place at the final stage, when you are satisfied with the overall content and organisation. It is your responsibility to make your writing clear and coherent, and, anyway, you are unlikely to find someone who is an expert in your scientific field, so it would be unwise (as well as unethical!) to ask them to do anything which would change the content or organisation of your text; the proofreader's role should be to check for surface errors in grammar and punctuation, or to make the phraseology more natural and idiomatic – without changing your meaning. A proofreader should only make suggestions; the final decision should always be yours.

The following reflective and review tasks will help you to consolidate your understanding of Chapter 2.

■ Reflective Task

1) How do you usually approach a writing task? What do you usually do first? What order do you usually do things in? How do you allocate time to the different stages of the writing process?

2) Does this way of doing things work well for you? Are there any new strategies you feel you would like to try out after reading this chapter?

■ Review Task

1) Go to your university website and find out if your department provides examples of previous assignment tasks or sample answers.

2) Think about how you might approach these assignments tasks and compare with the approach taken in any sample answers provided.

3) Select a text that you have written or are in the process of writing.

4) Proofread the text with reference to the proofreading activity in this chapter.

In this chapter, we have looked at what it means to write at university and ways of developing and improving your writing skills. We have explored the writing process and strategies for approaching the different stages of that process. In the next chapter, we will start to look at the language choices you will make as you write and edit a text.

References

Massey University. *Command words*. Available at: https://owll.massey.ac.nz/academic-writing/command-words.php (accessed 1st March, 2021).

Monash University. *Assignment direction words*. Available at: www.monash.edu/rlo/research-writing-assignments/understanding-the-assignment/assignment-direction-words (accessed 1st March, 2021).

Swales, J. and Feak, C. (2012) *Academic writing for graduate students: Essential tasks and skills* (3rd edition). Ann Arbor, MI: Michigan ELT.

Woodford, P. (1967) Sounder thinking through clearer writing. *Science*, 156(3776), 743–745.

Scientific style

This chapter will help you to become more familiar with the features of scientific style. It focuses on the importance of clarity and readability, and provides tips on how to produce writing which is concise and precise. It also explores the issue of register in scientific writing. Finally, it begins to look at some of the particular language features and conventions writers employ in scientific texts. This chapter primarily aims to help you make more informed choices when it comes to the words and phrases you use in your own writing.

1 What is good scientific style?

The term 'scientific style' is used here to refer to the style used in 'scientific writing', as defined in Chapter 1. It therefore describes the style of writing used by scientists to communicate with other scientists. This includes the written assignments that you may be required to produce as part of your scientific studies at university.

Scientific writing is most effective when it is:

- Clear and easy to read;
- Concise and precise;
- Neutral or formal in style.

These characteristics interconnect with each other: neutral, concise, precise language is likely to be clearer and easier to read. These are characteristics which are desirable in most forms of academic and professional writing. However, it could be argued that clarity, conciseness and precision are particularly important in science, where there is a need to build trust around issues which impact greatly on society. Using language which is clear and precise increases

DOI: 10.4324/9781003118572-4

transparency and decreases potential misunderstanding. Concise writing helps to focus the reader on the message, rather than distracting or hindering them with unnecessary traffic. A clear, readable text may also be said to be inclusive, in the sense that it is accessible to the widest possible range of readers. These issues relate to many current debates on the importance of clear communication in science, both among scientists and with the broader public.

When we talk about the degree of formality in a text, we are talking about the 'register' of a text. The term 'register' refers to the particular language we use in specific situations. For example, a job application is usually written in a formal register; a text message to a friend is usually written in an informal register; a contract is written in a legal register; a lab report is written in a scientific register; legal and scientific registers may also be seen as formal registers. As a science student, you will usually be required to write in a neutral/formal scientific resister. However, you could also be asked to write slightly more informal texts such as reflections, as discussed in Chapter 1. Furthermore, you need to be aware of the particular discourse practices in your own subject. There can be differences between writing styles across scientific disciplines. Some disciplines differ in terms of how direct they are, for example, or in their use of personal pronouns.

1.1 Clarity and readability

Although the scientific content of the texts you write at university may be complex and intellectually challenging, the texts themselves should be as clear and readable as possible. Many factors contribute to clarity, and some of them will be discussed in other sections of this chapter and in other chapters. In this section, we will focus on sentence length and organisation of information.

■ Explorative Task

Read the two texts that follow. Which one is easier to read? Match the texts to one of the descriptions in the table which follows to help you think about why this might be.

■ Text A

Telecommunications engineering is a discipline that brings together electrical engineering and computer science in order to enhance telecommunications systems. The work involved ranges from basic circuit design to strategic mass developments. The work of a telecommunications engineer includes designing and overseeing the installation of telecommunications equipment such as complex electronic switching systems, copper wire telephone facilities and fibre optics.

■ Text B

The discipline of telecommunications engineering, including the designing and installation overseeing of telecommunications equipment and facilities, such as complex electronic switching systems, copper wire telephone facilities and fibre optics, is the enhancement of telecommunication systems through the bringing together of electrical engineering and computer science, from basic circuit design to strategic mass developments.

1) Text _____	2) Text _____
is one very long sentence	is broken up into shorter sentences
has only one main verb (underline this)	has three sentences, each with a main verb (underline these)
gives a general definition near the end of the text, after specific details and examples have been given	begins with a general definition, followed by specific details and examples

Most people find Text A easier to read because:

- It moves from a general point to specific details, a common way of organising information (▶ **Chapter 6**).
- It is made up of fairly short sentences, each with a clear subject ('telecommunications engineering'; 'the work involved'; 'the work of a telecommunications engineer') and verb ('is'; 'ranges'; 'involves').

STUDY BOX: LONG OR SHORT SENTENCES?

It is sometimes thought that using very long sentences automatically makes a text more academic, but this is not the case. Most academic writing is usually a combination of long and short sentences, though this does depend on the subject or text focus. Short sentences can be used to good effect in scientific writing since they can convey information very clearly, as we saw in Text A. Long sentences can also be useful as they allow information to be combined. However, any long sentences used must be carefully controlled (▶ **Chapter 4** and **Chapter 5**), and not just amount to a string of loosely connected words and phrases. Long sentences should not be difficult to process. Most people find the very long sentence which makes up Text B quite hard to follow, even though it is grammatically correct.

■ Practice Task

Rewrite the text that follows so that it is clearer. Think about sentence length and organisation of information.

Paediatrics is a branch of medicine that deals with the care of infants, children and adolescents, the main differences between paediatric and adult medicine being the differences in physiology and legal status, with children unable to make decisions for themselves. Paediatricians usually deal with children from birth to eighteen years of age.

► **Model Text 2, Appendix 4**

The next sections will look at how to make writing as concise and precise as possible, thus enhancing the clarity of a text. Other factors which contribute to clarity are discussed in other chapters:

► **Chapter 2** discusses the importance of engaging with the writing process to clarify thinking and refine expression
► **Chapter 4 and Chapter 5** focus on the importance of using good sentence structure and punctuation to achieve clear expression
► **Chapter 6 and Chapter 8** explain how to develop clear paragraphs and texts
► **Chapter 9** looks at how following certain conventions of academic and scientific writing can help make a text easier to follow

1.2 Being concise

Scientific writing should be as concise as possible. This means not using more words than you have to. Writing which is not concise can sometimes be criticised as 'wordy' (using more words than is necessary), and this can sometimes involve 'redundancy' (the unnecessary repetition of words). Wordiness and redundancy can be distracting and confusing for the reader, and are often a sign that the writer is not in full control of the development of ideas in a text. Making a text more concise should form part of the write-read-write cycle that we discussed in Chapter 2: as you use the writing process to clarify your thinking and refine your expression, your text should become more concise.

■ Practice Task (i)

Rewrite these sentences to make them more concise.

1) All of the studies had limitations.

2) Scientists need to find solutions to solve these problems.

3) He makes a comparison of both the two systems.

4) In the conclusion part of the chapter, she reiterates the importance and significance of the results.

5) Pollution is a global problem throughout the world.

■ Practice Task (ii)

1) Look at the student's first draft of a report on a Chemistry MSc Research and Communications module at the University of Manchester and the lecturer's comments which follow.

A number of technological methods of extraction of copper are available, which include hydrometallurgy, solvent extraction, liquid-liquid electrochemistry and electrowinning. Liquid-liquid electrochemistry is the focus of this project. Each of these processes is described below and liquid-liquid electrochemistry is given greater consideration as it is the focus of this project.

"Accurate and well expressed – could be a little more concise, however."

2) Rewrite the text so that it is a little more concise.

3) Compare your text with the student's second draft.

▶   **Model Text 3, Appendix 4**

1.3 Being precise
Scientific writing should be precise. This means choosing words and phrases very carefully so that they convey your exact meaning. This entails being explicit and including everything that the reader needs in order to understand what you are saying. Writing which is not precise can be criticised as being vague or ambiguous. Achieving precision is a part of the write-read-write cycle we discussed in Chapter 2. Each word or phrase choice that you make will need to be carefully considered as you refine your understanding and expression. The language choices available to you will depend on your specific writing context. However, there are some general measures that you can take to improve the precision of your writing, as outlined in the Study Box that follows.

STUDY BOX: PRECISION IN WRITING

1) Avoid using 'etc.' or 'and so on'. Use 'such as' instead when you want to give just two or three examples, e.g.

cancer, diabetes, etc.

→ diseases **such as** cancer and diabetes

2) Avoid vague use of prepositions; instead, use common collocations (words which often go together) and fixed phrases with precise meaning, e.g.

For applications, nanotechnology has huge potential.

→ **In terms of** applications, nanotechnology has huge potential.

There are a number of factors of climate.

→ There are a number of **factors affecting** climate.

There are many problems of excessive alcohol consumption.

→ There are many **problems associated with** excessive alcohol consumption.

(= problems that arise when someone consumes too much alcohol)

Compare with:

the problem of excessive alcohol consumption

(= excessive alcohol consumption is a problem)

■ Practice Task (i)

Identify any vague language in these sentences and try to make them more precise and explicit.

1) The regulations cover the use of oil, gas, etc.

2) Buildings in the city are constructed of concrete, timber and so on.

3) For applications, this polymer is very versatile.

4) There are a number of factors of blood pressure.

5) There are many problems of obesity.

■ Practice Task (ii)

Choose the word or phrase which conveys the most precise meaning in the sentences that follow.

1) Over the years, robotics has **grown/evolved** to the point where there are now many intelligent machines that can carry out tasks autonomously.

2) One treatment option is minimally **invasive/intrusive** surgery.

3) The study surveyed civil engineers to **determine/decide** their reasons for entering the profession.

4) People **having/exhibiting** symptoms of Covid-19 should self-isolate.

5) Pharmacists are able to **administer/give** the vaccine.

6) The study reports on a simple **diagnosis/diagnostic** test for the disease.

7) The livestock sector has a high impact **for/in terms of** carbon footprint.

8) He discussed the adverse health effects **of/associated with** pollution.

1.4 Register

We all adopt different styles – or registers – depending on the situation. We try to speak politely and carefully in a job interview; we use relaxed – or sometimes 'colourful' – language among friends. The university context is no less complex. The degree of formality varies depending on the type of communication: an oral presentation will be less formal in style than a written research paper; a written reflection will have a more personal style than a lab report. So, the register and language choices you make while writing at university will depend on factors we discussed in some detail in Chapter 1 and Chapter 2: situation, audience and purpose.

As with most academic writing, scientific writing usually requires a neutral or formal style. This means that while informal expressions like 'lots of' are usually avoided, there is more flexibility when choosing between a neutral word like 'many' and a more academic expression such 'a considerable number of', and you may indeed vary between the two in academic texts.

The Practice Task that follows is just intended to get you to start thinking about degrees of formality and how you might use a dictionary to check on the register of a word.

Dictionaries often indicate register, as in the example in Figure 3.1:

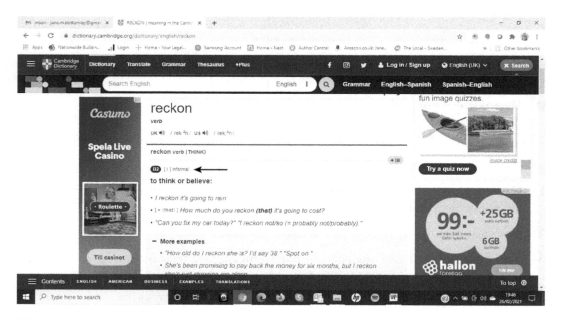

Figure 3.1 Cambridge Dictionary

■ Practice Task

Use a dictionary like the online Cambridge Dictionary to decide which of the underlined expressions would usually be too informal in academic writing.

1) The company **reckon/think/believe** that this software could revolutionise the industry.

2) Most of the **infants/children/kids** were inoculated.

3) The government provided **a great deal of/a considerable amount of/loads of** money for the project.

4) The conditions are **extremely difficult/very difficult/really difficult**.

5) The study looked into the effects of small amounts of **booze/liquor/alcohol** on the foetus.

■ Practice Task

As discussed, the issue of formality in texts is not straightforward. Some words and phrases are clearly inappropriate in formal texts, but sometimes, both neutral and formal options are available, and it is a matter of choice. Sometimes a slightly informal word or phrase will have a particular meaning that is difficult to convey in any other way. Read the text and reflect on the questions which follow, then try to rewrite the text so that it retains the same meaning, but is more formal in style.

> An autonomous vehicle is a vehicle that can sense its surroundings and move without much human input. People sometimes give them other names like 'self-drive cars', 'driverless cars' and even 'robocars'. Autonomous vehicles have some sensors to get a feel of the surroundings. They also have advanced control systems which figure out sensory information to pick out good navigation paths, as well as obstacles and relevant signs. There has been lots of hype about driverless cars in recent years, but progress in the field has been a bit slow.

Here are some questions to help you think about how you might make the text more formal:

1) Some words and phrases are quite informal and not usually used in formal writing. Can you identify some of these in the text and replace them with more formal options?

2) Academic writers may use the word 'good' but they often choose a word which is more precise. How could you change 'good navigation paths' to be more precise?

3) Can you think how you might make the phrases 'autonomous cars have' or they have' slightly more formal or technical?

4) Phrases like 'can sense' and 'can handle' are neutral and appropriate in a formal context, but can you think of options which have the same meaning but are slightly more formal?

5) Starting a sentence with 'People . . .' is rather too personal for a formal context. Can you think of a more formal way to write this sentence?

6) The 'to-infinitive' can convey purpose in all types of communication. Sometimes using the slightly more formal 'in order to' can enhance clarity. Is there a place in this text where the addition of this phrase might make the text slightly clearer?

7) The words 'surroundings' and 'signs' are appropriate in formal writing, but can you think of slightly more formal options?

8) The word 'hype' may seem rather informal. However, some would argue that it has a very precise meaning that would be lost if it was replaced. Can you think of a word which is close in meaning? Which word do you think is the better choice here? Can you change the word following 'hype' in this text to increase the formality of the phrase?

9) Rewrite the text to make it more formal in style then compare with the Model Text.

▶ **Model Text 4, Appendix 4**

2 Comparing academic and non-academic registers in science

The following task will allow you to compare different registers in a range of texts dealing with science. It will enable you to understand more about what differentiates academic style from other styles of writing in science. It will also introduce some of the particular language and conventions associated with academic writing.

■ Explorative Task

1) Read through the following texts quite quickly, without using a dictionary – it is not necessary to understand every word for this task – and decide whether you think they come from an academic or non-academic source.

■ Text A

The basic particles of which atoms are composed are the proton, the electron and the neutron. Some key properties of the proton, electron, and neutron are given in Table 1.4. A neutron and a proton have approximately the same mass and, relative to these, the electron has a negligible mass. The charge on a proton is of equal magnitude, but opposite sign, to that on an electron and so the combination of equal numbers of protons and electrons results in an assembly that is neutral overall. A neutron, as its name suggests, is neutral – it has no charge.

■ Text B

It sounds like an unusual way to win a Nobel Prize.

But ordinary sticky tape was crucial to the breakthrough that yielded graphene, a material with amazing properties and – potentially – numerous practical applications.

Graphene is a flat layer of carbon atoms tightly packed into a two-dimensional honey-comb arrangement.

It is both the thinnest and the strongest material known to science, and it conducts electricity better than copper.

This year's winners of the physics prize, Andre Geim and Konstantin Novoselov, from Manchester University, UK, extracted graphene from the common material known as graphite – widely used as lead in pencils.

Placing the adhesive tape on graphite, they managed to rip off thin flakes of carbon.

In the beginning they got flakes consisting of many layers of graphene.

But as they repeated the process many times, the flakes got thinner.

■ Text C

Microorganisms are used to recycle water during sewage treatment (Figure 1.7), converting the waste into useful byproducts such as CO_2, nitrates, phosphates, sulphates, ammonia, hydrogen sulphide and methane. Microbes have been routinely used for bioremediation since 1988, cleaning up toxic waste generated in a variety of industrial processes. In these cases, the organisms use the toxic waste as a source of energy, and in the process they decon-taminate it. They can also clean up underground wells, chemical spills and oil spills as well as producing useful products such as enzymes that are widely used in cleaning solutions.

■ Text D

One of Faraday's greatest intellectual innovations was the idea of force fields. These days, thanks to books and movies about bug-eyed aliens and their starships, most people are famil-iar with the term, so maybe he should get a royalty. But in the centuries between Newton and Faraday one of the great mysteries of physics was that its laws seemed to indicate that forces act across the empty space that separates interacting objects. Faraday didn't like that. He believed that to move an object, something has to come in contact with it. And so he imagined the space between electric charges and magnets as being filled with invisible tubes that physically do the pushing and pulling. Faraday called those tubes a force field.

■ Text E

Buildings in the city of Adapazari, Turkey, suffered heavy damage during the 1999 Mar-mara earthquake. Much of the devastation was attributed to the failure of the low plasticity non-plastic silts (Donahue *et al.* 2007) that had been deposited by the Sakarya River in its almost annual flooding of the plain over the past 7,000 years (Bol *et al.* 2010). The flood waters often did not recede for a considerable time, and they occasionally formed lakes.

■ Text F

In December, philosopher and artificial intelligence expert Aaron Sloman announced his intention to create nothing less than a robot mathematician. He reckons he has identified a key component of how humans develop mathematical talent. If he's right, it should be possible to program a machine to be as good as us at mathematics, and possibly better.

Sloman's creature is not meant to be a mathematical genius capable of advancing the frontiers of mathematical knowledge: his primary aim, outlined in the journal *Artificial Intelligence* (vol 172, p 2015), is to improve our understanding of where our mathematical ability comes from. Nevertheless, it is possible that such a robot could take us beyond what mathematicians have achieved so far. Forget robot vacuum cleaners and android waitresses; we're talking about a machine that could spawn a race of cyber-nerds capable of creating entirely new forms of mathematics.

■ **Text G**

Recently, Flaherty *et al.*[9] published the results of a questionnaire on older outpatients' use of alternative therapies in the US and Japan. According to their data, 74.3% of older Japanese outpatients had used at least one alternative therapy in the past 12 months: 22.0% had used herbs, 7.3% had used acupuncture, and 5.3% had used chiropractic.

■ **Text H**

Overweight and obesity are major threats to public health globally. One estimate suggests that 1.46 billion adults worldwide were overweight in 2008,[1] and projections suggest that by 2020 over 70% of adults in the United Kingdom and United States will be overweight.[2] This is likely to result in millions of additional cases of diabetes and heart disease and thousands of additional cases of cancer.[2]

2) What differences do you notice between the academic and non-academic texts? Some of these differences will be explored in the following section.

3 Common features of academic texts

In section 1, we discussed the features of good scientific style, i.e. style characterised by being clear, readable, concise, precise, and neutral or formal. The academic texts earlier are also characterised by particular language and conventions. The following Explorative Task will help you to identify examples of some of these.

■ **Explorative Task**

Match the features of academic scientific writing style (A) to examples of language and conventions in the examples (B) taken from the texts in the previous Exploratory Task.

■ **A**
Language and conventions

1) Academic texts use cautious language when necessary, often in order to avoid overgeneralisations.

   Find examples of cautious language: _____

2) They tend to adopt an impersonal style, making frequent use of passive constructions (► **Appendix 1**), and mostly avoiding the use of the personal pronouns 'I', 'we' and 'you'.

Find examples of passive constructions: _____

3) They use academic and technical language, or language which is neutral or formal in style. They avoid informal or colourful language. (► **Chapter 1**)

Find examples of technical language: _____

4) They use particular punctuation patterns, for example, making use of colons and semicolons to organise ideas (► **Chapter 5**), and mostly avoiding informal punctuation devices such as contractions, dashes and exclamation marks.

Find an example of colon use: _____

5) They contain references to sources, following standard referencing conventions (► **Chapter 9**). They tend not to include detailed bibliographic information in the main text, as is often the case in popular science writing.

Find examples of two styles of academic referencing: _____

6) They follow established academic conventions with regard to the use of tables and figures. (► **Chapter 9**)

Find examples of references to tables and figures: _____

■ B
Example texts

a) A neutron and a proton have approximately the same mass . . .

b) This is likely to result in millions of additional cases of diabetes and heart disease and thousands of additional cases of cancer.[2]

c) Some key properties of the proton, electron, and neutron are given in Table 1.4.

d) According to their data, 74.3% of older Japanese outpatients had used at least one alternative therapy in the past 12 months: 22.0% had used herbs, 7.3% had used acupuncture, and 5.3% had used chiropractic.

e) . . . deposited by the Sakarya River in its almost annual flooding of the plain over the past 7,000 years (Bol *et al.* 2010).

f) Much of the devastation has been attributed to the failure of the low plasticity non-plastic silts . . .

g) Microorganisms are used to recycle water during sewage treatment (Figure 1.7) . . .

Note that the line between academic and non-academic style is not always clearly drawn. As you can see from the earlier texts, academic texts contain occasional informal features such as dashes, e.g.

> A neutron, as its name suggests, is neutral – it has no charge.

And the non-academic texts can be academic in tone, e.g.

> Graphene is a flat layer of carbon atoms tightly packed into a two-dimensional honeycomb arrangement.

Journalistic language in science is often a combination of technical or academic language, and stylised, colloquial language. This reflects its aim to combine seriousness and objectivity with an engaging or entertaining delivery.

1) Cautious language

Cautious language has an important function. It allows you, for example, to express the limits of your knowledge or to qualify your claims. The use of this cautious language is known as 'hedging', i.e. the softening of language to avoid making assertions which cannot be substantiated (supported with evidence). If, however, you *are* able to substantiate claims, then your language needs to reflect this. Moreover, there are times when you need to express strong conviction, as opposed to caution, and this requires a different kind of language use, known as 'boosting'. Compare the following claims:

> The vaccine may be effective. (I believe that the evidence is not conclusive.)
> The vaccine is effective. (I believe that the evidence is conclusive.)
> The vaccine is most definitely effective. (I wish to convey my strong conviction that the evidence leaves no room for doubt.)

2) Personal pronouns

Personal pronouns are common in reflective writing but sometimes avoided in more formal academic writing. However, in some disciplines and journals, researchers prefer the pronoun 'we' to report on research. Note the example of Text G in Chapter 1:

> Using an age-structured transmission dynamic model, **we explored** different scenarios for COVID-19 transmission and control in the general population of the UK. **We found that** moderate interventions lasting for 12 weeks, such as school closures, self-isolation of symptomatic individuals, or shielding of older people, would probably not have been sufficient to control the epidemic and to avoid far exceeding available ICU capacity, even when these measures were used in combination.

It is best to have an open mind about this issue and to try to find out as much as you can about what is expected or preferred in your school or department.

As is clear from the discussion so far:

- There is a degree of variation in academic texts in terms of formality.
- You can often choose between neutral and more formal language in your own writing, but should mostly avoid informal language.

The following Study Box outlines some of ways of avoiding informality or increasing formality.

STUDY BOX: AVOIDING INFORMALITY; INCREASING FORMALITY

1) Single word negatives 'none/few/little' have a more formal tone than 'not + any/many/much', e.g.

  At the time, not many women worked in this area of science.

  → At the time, **few** women worked in this area of science.

  Not much research has been carried out on this topic.

  → **Little** research has been carried out on this topic.

Note that 'few' is used with countable nouns and 'little' with uncountable nouns.

Be careful not to confuse with 'a few/a little', meaning 'some' or 'a small number/amount'.

▶ **Appendix 3** on 'fewer' and 'less'

2) In formal writing, adverbs are often placed before the main verb, rather than at the beginning (or sometimes the end) of a sentence, as is common in spoken English, e.g.

  Originally, the research was conducted in China.

  → The research was **originally** conducted in China.

  Then the tube was placed in the furnace.

  → The tube was **then** placed in the furnace.

3) Note that, in academic texts, it is generally considered better to avoid the use of 'and' and 'but' at the start of a sentence. However, it is only really a problem if you *overuse* these words to start a sentence, as this can make the text seem unstructured or 'chatty'. Occasionally starting sentences this way is not a problem and may sometimes even be a good choice.

4) You can usually replace 'get', 'about', 'though' and 'like' with more formal equivalents, e.g.

> Brown got a Nobel Prize for his work on boranes.

> → Brown **received/earned/was awarded** a Nobel Prize for his work on boranes.

> about **200** people

> → **approximately/an estimated** 200 people

> Though cooking may destroy the bacterial cells, it is unlikely to inactivate the toxin.

> → **Although** cooking may destroy the bacterial cells, it is unlikely to inactivate the toxin.

> devices like smart phones and tablets

> → devices **such as** smart phones and tablets

5) You can make a text more formal by replacing these expressions with 'get/make/do' with more formal equivalents:

> get worse → deteriorate

> do better → improve

> make easier → facilitate

6) Be careful when using 'besides' and 'as well'. Used alone, they have a conversational tone; they have a more formal tone when followed by a noun or -*ing* form, e.g.

> The dye is used in the textile industry. Besides, it has applications in food production.

> → **Besides being used** in the textile industry, the dye has applications in food production.

> The dye has applications in the food industry as well.

> → **As well as being used** in the textile industry, the dye has applications in the food industry.

7) Avoid conversational expressions such as *actually, by the way* or *to be honest*.

> Actually, the results concur with this study.

> → **In fact**, the results concur with this study.

8) Avoid the informal expressions 'lots of' ('a lot of' is a little informal, but sometimes used in academic writing) and 'loads of', e.g.

Lots of studies back up these findings.

→ **Many/A large number of/A considerable number of** studies back up these findings.

The earlier expressions should only be used with countable nouns; use the expressions that follow with uncountable nouns:

a large amount of/a considerable amount of/a great deal of time/money/research

9) It is usually best to avoid informal punctuation such as contractions, dashes and exclamation marks.

■ Practice Task (i)

Identify examples of informal style in these examples from the texts analysed earlier in the chapter.

1) . . . we're talking about a machine that could spawn a race of cyber-nerds . . .

2) It sounds like an unusual way to win a Nobel Prize.

3) . . . they got flakes consisting of many layers of graphene . . .

4) . . . bug-eyed aliens and their starships . . .

5) He reckons he has identified a key component of how humans develop mathematical talent.

6) And so he imagined the space between electric charges and magnets as being filled with invisible tubes that physically do the pushing and pulling.

7) . . . a material with amazing properties and – potentially – numerous practical applications . . .

8) Faraday didn't like that.

9) . . . Andre Geim and Konstantin Novoselov, from Manchester University, UK . . .

10) . . . his primary aim, outlined in the journal *Artificial Intelligence* (vol 172, p 2015) . . .

■ Practice Task (ii)

Which of these sentences, a) or b), is more typical of an academic text? Why? Note that all the sentences are grammatically correct, and could possibly feature in academic texts, but one is more academic in style than the other.

1)

    a)   The first clinical trial was conducted in 2008.

    b)   We conducted the first clinical trial in 2008.

2)

    a)   There are three main treatments for cancer – surgery, radiation therapy and chemotherapy.

    b)   There are three main treatments for cancer: surgery, radiation therapy and chemotherapy.

3)

    a)   Mobile phone use poses a danger to health.

    b)   Mobile phone use may pose a danger to health.

4)

    a)   Not many materials exhibit strong magnetism.

    b)   Few materials exhibit strong magnetism.

5)

    a)   Rutherford received the Nobel Prize in Chemistry in 1908.

    b)   Rutherford got the Nobel Prize in Chemistry in 1908.

6)

    a)   There are about 3,000 species of cricket in the world.

    b)   There are approximately 3,000 species of cricket in the world.

7)

    a)   An increasing number of seals are being treated for internal problems caused by oil poisoning.

    b)   More and more seals are being treated for internal problems caused by oil poisoning.

8)

    a)   The machine was originally developed for internal company research.

    b)   Originally, the machine was developed for internal company research.

■ Practice Task (iii)

Rewrite these sentences to make them more academic in style, without changing the meaning or emphasis. Most sentences only require minor changes.

1) In the beginning they got flakes consisting of many layers of graphene. But as they repeated the process many times, the flakes got thinner.

_____

2) He reckons he has identified a key component of how humans develop mathematical talent.

_____

3) This study aims to figure out what caused the structural damage.

_____

4) A lot of research has been done on the subject of runway friction.

_____

5) Most thermometers are closed glass tubes containing liquids like alcohol or mercury.

_____

6) Then, the solution was heated to about 70°C.

_____

7) You can see the results of the analysis in Table 2.

_____

8) Not much is known about the proteins linked with RNA.

_____

9) Eating disorders cause individuals to feel tired and depressed.

_____

10) There are three different types of volcano – active volcanoes (erupt frequently), dormant volcanoes (temporarily inactive but not fully extinct), and extinct volcanoes (unlikely to erupt again).

_____

■ Review Task

*Summarise the information in Text B, presenting it in a more academic style. You will need to think about organisation of information as well as language. Use your own words as much as possible, but do not try to change technical language (▶ **Chapter** 7 for more information on this last point).*

▶   **Model Text 5, Appendix 4**

STUDY BOX: VOCABULARY RESOURCES

1) Dictionaries

As well as definitions, dictionaries, particularly those designed for language learners, such as Cambridge Dictionary, provide information on the special characteristics of words, including their register, grammar and usage. The Oxford Learner's Dictionary of Academic English focuses on words and phrases common in academic English, providing very useful information on usage in academic writing.

2) Thesauruses

A thesaurus can be a useful tool but like any tool it requires careful, critical use. The synonyms presented may not be exact synonyms, and they may in fact be quite different in terms of register and usage. Also, remember that it is not always a good idea to vary the terms you use. Sometimes repetition is the right choice, especially for key words and technical terms. We will see in Chapter 6 how repetition can be an important cohesive device, helping the reader to navigate the text.

3) Academic Word List

The Academic Word List is a list of words which occur at a high frequency in English-language academic texts. It is a useful resource if you want to check if a word is academic in style.

The following reflective and review tasks will help you to consolidate your understanding of Chapter 3.

■ Reflective Task

1) How do you try to make your writing as clear, concise and precise as possible? Are there any new strategies that you feel you would like to try out after reading this chapter?

2) Think about the last three things you have written in English. This might include assignments, notes, emails, letters, text messages or tweets. How did the language choices you made fit the register of these texts?

■ Review Task

1) Select a text that you have written or are in the process of writing.

2) Try to improve the text by focusing on style.

In this chapter, we have explored the characteristics of scientific style. In the next chapter, we will start to look at sentence structure.

Sources of example texts

Arel, E. and Önalp, A. (2012) Geotechnical properties of Adapazari silt. *Bulletin of Engineering Geology and the Environment*, 71, 709–720.

Brooks, M. (2009) Rise of the robogeeks. In *New Scientist*, 3rd March. Available at: www.newscientist.com/article/mg20126971.800-rise-of-the-robogeeks.html (accessed 19th January, 2021).

Hawking, S. and Mlodinov, L. (2011) *The grand design: New answers to the ultimate questions of life*. New York: Bantam Books.

Housecroft, C. and Constable, E. (2010) *Chemistry: An introduction to organic, inorganic and physical chemistry* (4th edition). Harlow: Pearson Education.

Howard, S., Adams, J. and White, M. (2012) Nutritional content of supermarket ready meals and recipes by television chefs in the United Kingdom: Cross sectional study. *BMJ*, 2012; 345, e7607.

Rincon, P. (2011) How sticky tape led to the Nobel Prize. *BBC*, 5th October. Available at: www.bbc.co.uk/news/science-environment-11478645 (accessed 19th January, 2021).

Strelkauskas, A., Strelkauskas, J. and Moszyk-Strelkauskas, D. (2010) *Microbiology: A clinical approach*. Abingdon: Garland Science.

Yamashita, H., Tsukayama, H. and Sugishita, C. (2002) Popularity of complementary medicine in Japan: A telephone survey. *Complementary Therapies in Medicine*, 10, 84–93.

References

Academic Word List. Available at: www.wgtn.ac.nz/lals/resources/academicwordlist (accessed 11th December, 2020).

Cambridge Dictionary. Available at: https://dictionary.cambridge.org/ (accessed 12th January, 2021).

Oxford Learner's Dictionary of Academic English. Available at: www.oxfordlearnersdictionaries.com/definition/academic/ (accessed 27th January, 2021).

Sentence structure 1

This chapter will provide an overview of English sentence structure. It will help you to write clearer sentences by improving your understanding of how the 'building blocks' of sentences fit together. It will also demonstrate how different types of sentence can perform various functions in your writing. This includes examination of common structures in scientific writing, such as infinitives of purpose and relative clauses.

1 The 'heart' of a sentence: subject + verb structures

Most sentences in English are built around one or more **subject + verb** structures, where the verb agrees with the subject, e.g.

- **Heat capacity is** the ability to absorb and retain heat.

- **Deformation of concrete results** both from environmental effects, such as moisture gain or loss and heat, and from applied stress, both long- and short-term.

- **Bacteria are** the smallest living organisms.

- **Atoms**, the building blocks of elements, **consist** of a nucleus surrounded by a cloud of orbiting electrons.

DOI: 10.4324/9781003118572-5

- The concepts underlying the changing health needs, status and situations of groups $\overset{\text{S}}{\underline{\hspace{8cm}}}$

  $\underline{\underset{\text{V}}{\text{and nations}}\ \underset{}{\text{are becoming}}}$ ever better understood, and $\underline{\underset{\text{S}}{\text{terms to describe them}}}$

  $\underline{\underset{\text{V}}{\text{are changing}}}$.

Note that the subject can be made up of one or several words.

▶ **Appendix 2 Noun Phrases** for information on the structure and function of multi-word subjects
▶ **Appendix 1 Verb Forms** for information on verb forms

■ Explorative Task

*Identify the **subject + verb** structures in these sentences.*

1) Lime (CaO) is widely used as an ingredient in mortars, plasters and masonry.

2) One of the most noticeable trends over many decades has been shifting patterns of health and especially the causes of morbidity (illness) and mortality (death).

3) A motherboard is the major circuit board inside a computer and it holds the processor, the computer bus, the main memory and many other vital components.

4) Solar power is one facet of renewable energy, with wind and geothermal being others.

5) Although quarantine is the oldest method of dealing with communicable diseases, it is now generally used only for very severe diseases, such as cholera and yellow fever.

2 Sentence types

In English, **subject + verb** structures occur in three main types of sentence.

■ Explorative Task

Look again at some of the sentences from section 1.

- *Which ones have more than one **subject + verb** structure?*
- *How are they linked together? What is the relationship between the two parts of the sentence?*

1) Bacteria are the smallest living organisms.

2) A motherboard is the major circuit board inside a computer and it holds the processor, the computer bus, the main memory and many other vital components.

3) Although quarantine is the oldest method of dealing with communicable diseases, it is now generally used only for very severe diseases, such as cholera and yellow fever.

The three main sentence types exemplified here are: **simple** (1) (with only one subject + verb structure), **compound** (2) and **complex** (3) (both with two subject + verb structures*). These sentence types will be discussed in more detail in the following sections.

*Compound and complex sentences can also be formed in other ways, as will be discussed later in the chapter.

2.1 Forming simple sentences

Simple sentences consist of a single **main clause**, i.e. they are built around a single **subject + verb** structure. As well as containing a **subject**, and a **verb** which agrees with the subject, a main clause can also contain:

- An **object** (who or what is affected by the verb), e.g.
  - The university funded **the study**.
  - The group researched **the causes of diabetes**.
- A **complement** (information about the subject or object of the clause), e.g.
  - She is **a doctor**.
  - They made him **head of department**.
- An **adverbial** (information about the situation), e.g.
  - The book has **undoubtedly** contributed to the debate on climate change.
  - **In the early 20th century**, many advances were made in the field of physics.
  - **When conducting trials on mice**, they found the drug to be effective and harmless.

Note that subjects, objects and complements are usually noun phrases. However, some other elements, such as subordinate clauses (▶ **2.2** for an explanation of subordinate clauses), can also take on these functions, e.g.

What Darwin did changed the way we understand biology.

See the earlier examples, where adverbs ('undoubtedly'), prepositional phrases ('In the early 20th century') and subordinate clauses ('When conducting trials on mice') function as adverbials.

■ Explorative Task

*Underline extra words or phrases that have been added to the main **subject + verb** structure in each of the simple sentences that follow. What is the grammar/function of these words and phrases?*

1) Temperatures rose.

2) Temperatures rose steadily.

3) Average temperatures in the south of the country rose steadily.

4) In the period from 2003 to 2013, average temperatures in the south of the country rose steadily.

■ Practice Task

These sentences are not accurately formed. Can you identify the problems with them?

1) It undoubtedly true that computational simulations should not completely replace experimentation.

2) An ICT system is a set-up consists of hardware, software, data, and the people who use these things.

3) Vitamin D is important for the absorption and use of calcium and phosphorus by the body, it is essential for the formation and health of bones, teeth and cartilage.

2.2 Compound and complex sentences

As previously mentioned, compound and complex sentences often contain two **subject + verb** structures, i.e. **clauses**, but they combine them in different ways.

■ Explorative Task

Look again at these sentences from section 1.

- *In which sentence could the two clauses exist independently?*
- *In which sentence is one clause dependent on the other?*

1) A motherboard is the major circuit board inside a computer and it holds the processor, the computer bus, the main memory and many other vital components.

2) Although quarantine is the oldest method of dealing with communicable diseases, it is now generally used only for very severe diseases, such as cholera and yellow fever.

In 1), two facts are combined, but they are not dependent on each other here. If the sentence were split into two, there would be no change of meaning. They are independent **main clauses** joined by a **coordinating conjunction**, 'and', to form a **compound sentence**.

In 2), the **subordinating conjunction** 'although' introduces a dependent **subordinate clause**, which must be connected to a **main clause** for the sentence to make sense: the two facts (quarantine is the oldest method; it is not widely used now) are related here to form a **complex sentence**. If the subordinating element is removed, the link between the facts is not explicit.

A **compound-complex** sentence contains both coordinated and subordinated clauses, e.g.

-

| main clause 1 | coordinator | main clause 2 |

Vaccines against malaria have been sought for years but these have yet to be successful,

subordinate clause

although optimism surfaces regularly.

STUDY BOX: AVOIDING COMMON ERRORS AND STYLE PROBLEMS IN COMPOUND AND COMPLEX SENTENCES

1) Be careful not to duplicate conjunctions, e.g.

> **As** some of the drug's side effects may be difficult to detect **and** patients might take a long time to become aware of them. ✗

> **As** some of the drug's side effects may be difficult to detect, patients might take a long time to become aware of them. ✓

> Some of the drug's side effects may be difficult to detect **and** patients might take a long time to become aware of them. ✓

2) Be careful not to write just half a sentence when using subordinating conjunctions such as 'whereas' and 'because', e.g.

> Influenza B and C viruses mainly affect humans. Whereas influenza A viruses infect a range of mammalian and avian species. ✗

> Influenza B and C viruses mainly affect humans, whereas influenza A viruses infect a range of mammalian and avian species. ✓

3) Avoid 'stringy' sentences with lots of 'and's' and 'but's'. These tend to be wordy, unstructured and difficult to read.

> The weather conditions worsened and this caused a number of problems and there were forest fires and droughts but the long-term effects were limited. ✗

> The weather conditions worsened, which caused a number of problems including forest fires and droughts. However, the long-term effects were limited. ✓

■ Practice Task

Correct or improve these sentences.

1) Although the structure of the building was weakened, but experts agreed that there was no danger of it collapsing.

_____

2) The drug trial was abandoned. Because the side effects were considered to be too serious.

_____

3) The panda was artificially inseminated and experts claimed that her hormone and behavioural signs indicated that she was carrying a foetus but her behaviour changed and she is thought to have lost the cub.

_____

2.2.1 Forming compound sentences

The typical sentence pattern for compound sentences is:

subject + verb (. . .) + coordinating conjunction (and/but/or) + subject + verb (. . .)

•   A motherboard is the major circuit board inside a computer and it holds the processor, the computer bus, the main memory and many other vital components.

A comma is often used before the conjunction, e.g.

•   Obesity appears to have more negative health consequences than smoking, drinking or poverty, and it also affects more people.

This comma is known as an 'Oxford comma', and its use is sometimes disputed. However, it can often make a sentence clearer by separating elements and reducing the possibility of ambiguity. See 'Grammar's great divide: The Oxford comma' at TEDEd for an informative, entertaining explanation of this issue.

In compound sentences, when both clauses have the same subject, the subject of the second clause can often be omitted, e.g.

- Glass is resistant to most chemicals but can be dissolved by hydrofluoric acid.

However, it should be retained if there is any chance of ambiguity.

■ Practice Task

Link the sentence halves with the right coordinating conjunction to form compound sentences.

1 A poor diet can lead to obesity	and	a it has also brought with it a number of problems.
2 The hurricane destroyed a number of buildings	but	
	or	b injected.
3 The drug can be taken orally		c others show little improvement.
4 The Internet has improved our lives in many ways		d cause a number of health problems.
5 Some patients respond well to therapy		e caused major damage to trees.

1) _____

2) _____

3) _____

4) _____

5) _____

2.2.2 Forming complex sentences with subordinating conjunctions
Typical sentence patterns when using **subordinating conjunctions** are:

subordinating conjunction + subject + verb (. . .), + subject + verb (. . .)

(clauses usually separated by comma)

- <u>As soon as the liquid reaches the required temperature,</u> <u>it should be removed from</u> the heat.

      subordinate clause   main clause

Or

subject + verb (. . .) + subordinating conjunction + subject + verb (. . .)

(comma not usually used)

| main clause | subordinate clause |

- The liquid should be removed from the heat as soon as it reaches the required temperature.

The decision about the order of the main and subordinate clauses will depend on the context. Both structures are grammatically correct, and the order may often be unimportant in terms of meaning. However, sometimes the order will affect the meaning or emphasis of the sentence, or how it relates to what comes before or after in a text. It can also be related to the tendency in English for new and important information to be placed at the end of a sentence, which is discussed in more detail in Chapter 6.

Some common **subordinating conjunctions** used in academic writing are as follows:

- Indicating time, duration or sequence: *when; while; as; as soon as; since; until; before; after*
- Stating conditions: *if; unless; in case; provided that*
- Giving reasons: *because; since; as*
- Indicating result: *so; so that*
- Contrasting: *while; whilst; whereas*
- Indicating concession (allowing for something): *although; even though*

■ Practice Task (i)

Choose the correct subordinating conjunction.

1) Many people prefer natural remedies to conventional drugs **as/while** they believe natural remedies have fewer side effects.

2) **Because/Whereas** many buildings in the city are built to withstand earthquakes, some are still at considerable risk.

3) **Although/Since** the weather conditions were fairly good, they decided not to proceed with the test flight.

4) Mobile phones should be switched off **unless/in case** they interfere with emergency equipment.

5) Take the drug **as soon as/until** the symptoms occur.

■ Practice Task (ii)

Link the sentence halves and insert the correct subordinating conjunction to form complex sentences:

although; while; as; so that; whereas

1 it remains the case that the brain as a whole has limited powers of repair	a ___ measures may be taken to reduce the likelihood of future incidents.
2 The stability of glass makes disposal difficult	b it reaches upwards into biology for many of its extraordinary applications.
3 The reasons for developing type 1 diabetes have not been identified	c ___ some suggest interaction of dietary factors during pregnancy and early neonatal life.
4 ___ chemistry reaches down into physics for its explanations	d the potential use of stem cells offers new hope for future therapy for degenerative brain diseases.
5 It is sometimes necessary to acquire information regarding the cause of a ceramic fracture	e ___ it will not readily break down.

1) _____

2) _____

3) _____

4) _____

5) _____

2.3 Other complex sentences

There are a number of other subordinating mechanisms, many of which are common in academic writing. Some examples are discussed in the next section.

2.3.1 Participle clauses

The typical sentence pattern using participles is:

subject + verb (. . .), *-ed/-ing* (. . .)

-
  | main clause | participle clause |

  The banks of the river burst, leading to serious flooding.

  ——*ed/ing* (...), subject + verb (...)

The participle clause can also come first in the sentence, but this will depend on how the information fits into a broader text.

-
  | participle clause | main clause |

  Written in 1859, Darwin's *Origin of Species* revolutionised the study of biology.

■ Practice Task

Complete the sentences with one of the following verbs in a suitable form:

prompt; weigh; use; compose

1) The traffic light system is used on the front of packaging to help consumers assess at a glance the fat, saturated fat, sugar and salt content, _____ them to make healthier dietary choices.

2) The brain is a very complex structure, _____ of around one hundred thousand million (i.e. 10^{11}) neurons.

3) _____ matter before it had undergone transformation from one substance to another led to the principal concept that underlies all explanations in chemistry: the *atom*.

4) Inexpensive microelectronic circuits are mass produced by _____ some very ingenious fabrication techniques.

2.3.2 Infinitive clauses of purpose
Infinitive clauses of purpose are very common in scientific writing.

The typical sentence pattern is:

subject + verb (. . .) + infinitive clause

(comma not usually used)

- main clause _____ infinitive clause
Organic matter can be added to soil to lower the pH.

infinitive clause, + subject + verb (...)

(comma usually used)

- infinitive clause _____ main clause
To lower the pH of soil, organic matter can be added.

The infinitive clause can also come first in the sentence, usually followed by a comma.

The phrases 'in order to' and 'so as to' can also be used to introduce purpose.

- **in order to/so as to** lower the pH of soil

■ Practice Task

Link the sentence halves with the right verb to form complex sentences:

1 All structural concrete contains to reduce steel reinforcement in the form of bars or welded mesh	to reduce	a the weight and improve the performance of its aircraft.
2 We must understand the transmission mechanisms of infection so that we can interfere with those mechanisms	to take	b the low tensile strength of concrete.
3 Water is then added	to dilute	c suspects, and to analyse the scenes of crimes.
4 Stemming from analytical chemistry is *forensic chemistry*, in which the techniques of analytical chemistry are used for legal purposes	to compensate for	d the acid to 20–30% and the mixture is again heated to 100°C for 1 hour.
5 Aluminium-lithium alloys have been developed by the aircraft industry	to track down	e effective public health measures.

1) _____

2) _____

3) _____

4) _____

5) _____

This structure can be very useful in the methods section of a research report, often combined with the passive, e.g.

To obtain *the correct values of T_s (skin temperature) by compensating for the effects of different radiation sources the following parameters* **were supplied** *for the camera:* . . .

In order to allow acclimatisation, the thermograms **were recorded** after a 15-min stay in the respective environment.

To document the recurrence of thermal windows, we further partitioned each body part into three sections . . .

To document the relative size of a thermal window and to observe its chrono-logical development we used the software package ImageJ 1.36B . . .

To test for the influence of T_a, age, and body weight on T_s, we used linear mixed effect models . . .

(Weissenbock *et al.*, 2010: 183)

2.3.3 that-*clauses*

Many verbs (also some adjectives and nouns) introduce a subordinate clause with the conjunction 'that', e.g.

- The *First Law* of thermodynamics asserts **that** the total energy of the universe is constant and cannot be changed.

It is often possible to omit 'that' from the clause, but it is usually a good idea to retain it in academic writing as it can increase clarity.

■ Practice Task

Add the word 'that' to these sentences where necessary/preferable.

1) Immunisation requires we understand the immune mechanisms and we design vaccines that will successfully stimulate protection.

2) One estimate suggests 1.46 billion adults worldwide were overweight in 2008,[1] and projections suggest by 2020 over 70% of adults in the United Kingdom and United States will be overweight.

3) It is popularly believed the cells of wood are living cells, but this is certainly not the case.

4) Chemists take a great deal of interest in the rates of chemical reactions as there is little point knowing they can, in principle, generate a substance in a reaction but it would take a millennium to make a milligram.

5) Over time, it is becoming more apparent the earth is virtually a closed system relative to its constituent materials and its resources are finite.

2.4 Focus on relative clauses

Relative clauses are very common in academic writing. They are very useful in science as they can **specify** or **define** a particular object, e.g.

- A heavy metal is one **that has a high relative atomic mass**.

▶ **Chapter 8** for examples of relative clauses in definitions

Relative clauses can also **add information** to a statement, e.g.

- Heavy metals, **which include copper, lead, and zinc,** can be a cause of environmental pollution.

Relative clauses can cause difficulty because they are quite complex in terms of grammar and punctuation.

■ Explorative Task

Compare the relative clauses highlighted in the text. In what ways do they differ?

Since the start of the industrial revolution in the late 18th century, there has been an exponential increase in our exploitation of materials for use in the technologies **that have driven economic growth and increased the prosperity and living standards in much of the world**. These advances have not, of course, been uniformly experienced owing to the wide variation in political, economic and social conditions in different regions and countries. Much of the growth has only been possible with the associated development and fabrication of infrastructure, **which has required enormous quantities of construction materials with controlled and reliable properties**.

(Domone and Illston, 2010: 535)

DEFINING OR NON-DEFINING RELATIVE CLAUSE?

The first clause is a **defining** (or **'restrictive'**) relative clause. It **specifies** only those 'technologies' responsible for these effects; it does not refer to 'technologies' in general. Defining clauses can begin with 'that' or 'which' ('that' or 'who' for people). The second clause is a **non-defining/non-restrictive** clause. It refers to 'the development and growth of infrastructure' in general, adding some **extra information** rather than specifying a certain part of it. Non-defining clauses must begin with 'which' (or 'who' for people), and they must be separated from the main clause by a comma/commas.

■ Practice Task (i)

Complete the sentences with: 'that/which/who' and, if necessary, a comma/commas.

1) A computer virus is a program _____ can damage your computer.

2) Brisk walking is something _____ many doctors recommend to those _____ are overweight.

3) A marine engineer is someone _____ works with underwater equipment and systems.

4) Vitamin C _____ is also known as ascorbic acid is required by the body for the growth and repair of tissue.

5) Global warming leads to climate change _____ will ultimately affect people all over the world.

Sometimes, the relative pronoun of a defining relative clause can be omitted if it refers to the object, rather than the subject of a sentence. Compare:

- technologies that have driven economic growth
- technologies (that) industry has employed

Can any of the relative pronouns in the sentences in Practice Task (i) be omitted?

Relative clauses can also sometimes be further reduced (to form 'reduced relative clauses'), i.e. both the relative pronoun and auxiliary verb *to be* can be omitted, leaving just a past participle, e.g.

- This study shows that neither recipes **created** by popular television chefs nor ready meals **produced** by three leading UK supermarket chains meet national or international nutritional standards for a balanced diet.
- Highly educated people **living** in urban areas use more dietary supplements.

Can any of the sentences in Practice Task (i) be reduced?

Relative clauses with a preposition are also characteristic of formal writing, e.g.

- The ancient technique of 'stained glass', **in which** pigments were fired directly onto the surface of clear glass, has been updated recently.
- Bacteria and their products have been used extensively to control pests such as caterpillars, bollworms, corn borers, and fruit leaf rollers, **all of which** can damage crops used for food.
- The UK manufactures 750,000 tonnes of flat glass each year, **three quarters of which** goes into glazing products for buildings.

■ Practice Task (ii)

Add the correct preposition to the sentences in the correct place:

  at; of; above; in

1) There are several theories, most which have been discussed at length in the literature.

2) This is the paper which Maxwell's equations first appeared.

3) The line on the graph indicates the threshold which the reaction is deemed significant.

4) Note the rate which the solution heats up.

5) The plants produced pods, some which were green, and some which were yellow.

In possessive constructions, 'whose' is commonly used with inanimate objects in academic writing: Biber *et al.* (1999: 618) found that 75% of 'whose' in academic writing referred back to inanimate nouns, e.g.

> They realised that only another planet, **whose** orbit lay beyond those already recognised, could explain the behaviour of the nearer planets.

These constructions can also be written as more complex phrases. Compare:

> They realised that only another planet, **the orbit of which** lay beyond those already recognised, could explain the behaviour of the nearer planets.

■ Practice Task (iii)

Join these sentences together to form a single sentence containing a relative clause.

1) Arsenic is an extremely toxic substance. It is sometimes used as an insecticide.

    Arsenic _____

2) The Royal Society was founded in 1660. It is a self-governing fellowship of many of the world's most distinguished scientists.

    The Royal Society_____

3) The disease has a number of symptoms. Most of them can be controlled through medication.

    The disease _____

4) Technology can help countries to develop. It is unclear to what extent.

    The extent _____

5) Gravitational wave astronomy is an emerging new field of astronomy. It aims to use gravitational wave detectors to collect observational data about compact objects.

    Gravitational wave astronomy _____

6) A crystal is a piece of matter. Its boundaries are naturally formed plane surfaces.

    A crystal _____

7) Tim Berners-Lee invented the Internet. It was in 1989.

It was Tim Berners-Lee _____

8) Fracking is a procedure. A solution is pumped into the earth to fracture rock and access oil and gas.

Fracking_____

> Think about how you could use this technique to produce a simple **paraphrase** of original sources. ▶ **Chapter 7**

The following reflective and review tasks will help you to consolidate your understanding of Chapter 4.

■ Reflective Task

1) What do you find most difficult about sentence structure in English?

2) What are some of the differences between sentence structure in English and sentence structure in your first language?

■ Review Task

1) Select a text that you have written or are in the process of writing.

2) Try to improve the text by focusing on sentence structure.

> In this chapter, we have looked at the foundations of sentence structure. In the next chapter, we will look at different ways of combining elements in and between sentences and building complexity in a text.

Source of example texts

Atkins, P. (2013) *What is chemistry?* Oxford: Oxford University Press, pp 2, 6, 12, 17, 33, 39.

Domone, P. and Illston, J. (eds) (2010) *Construction materials: Their nature and behaviour*, Abingdon: Spon Press, pp 133, 189, 253, 407, 515, 516, 528, 546.

Housecroft, C. and Constable, E. (2010) *Chemistry: An introduction to organic, inorganic and physical chemistry* (4th edition). Harlow: Pearson Education, p 590.

Howard, S., Adams, J. and White, M. (2012) Nutritional content of supermarket ready meals and recipes by television chefs in the United Kingdom: Cross sectional study. *BMJ* 2012, 345, e7607.

Kuno, M. (2012) *Introductory nanoscience: Physical and chemical concepts*. Abingdon: Garland Science, p 420.

McCracken, K. and Phillips, D. (2012) *Global health: An introduction to current and future trends*. Abingdon: Routledge, pp 157, 165, 167.

Okasha, S. (2002) *Philosophy of science*. Oxford: Oxford University Press, pp 77.

OpenLearn. *Addiction and neural aging*. Available at: www.open.edu/openlearn/science-maths-technology/science/biology/addiction-and-neural-ageing/content-section-4.7 (accessed 27th February, 2021).

OpenLearn. *Computers and computing systems*. Available at: www.open.edu/openlearn/science-maths-technology/computing-ict/computers-and-computer-systems/content-section-3.2 (accessed 27th February, 2021).

Strelkauskas, A., Strelkauskas, J. and Moszyk-Strelkauskas, D. (2010) *Microbiology: A clinical approach*. Abingdon: Garland Science, pp 11, 19, 54, 108, 121, 195, 444, 699.

Weissenbock, N., Weiss, C., Schwammer, H. and Kratochvil, H. (2010) Thermal windows on the body surface of African elephants *(Loxodonta africana)* studied by infrared thermography. *Journal of Thermal Biology*, pp 35, 182–188, p 183.

Yamashita, H., Tsukayama, H. and Sugishita, C. (2002) Popularity of complementary medicine in Japan: A telephone survey. *Complementary Therapies in Medicine*, pp 10, 84–93, p 86.

References

Biber, D., Johansson, S., Leech, G., Conrad, S. and Finegan, E. (1999) *Longman grammar of spoken and written English*. Harlow: Pearson Education.

TEDEd. *Grammar's great divide: The Oxford comma*. Available at: https://ed.ted.com/lessons/grammar-s-great-divide-the-oxford-comma-ted-ed (accessed 27th February, 2021).

CHAPTER
5

Sentence structure 2

> This chapter will build on Chapter 4 by further exploring different ways of combining ideas, and thus building complexity in texts. It will also focus on punctuation, an aspect of language which can sometimes be neglected, but one which can greatly enhance the clarity and style of your writing.

1 Combining ideas

In Chapter 4, we looked at how clauses combine in sentences. In this chapter, we will look at how words and phrases can be used to link clauses, sentences and ideas.

■ Explorative Task

Consider the differences between the underlined elements in these sentences.

1) The drug was banned <u>because there were serious adverse side effects</u>.

2) The drug was banned <u>because of the serious adverse side effects</u>.

3) The drug had serious adverse side effects. <u>Because of the seriousness of these side effects</u>, the drug was banned.

4) The drug had serious adverse side effects. <u>Because of this</u>, it was banned.

5) The drug had serious adverse side effects. <u>Consequently</u>, it was banned.

6) The drug had serious side effects. <u>As a result</u>, it was banned.

DOI: 10.4324/9781003118572-6

This box presents the grammatical terminology used to describe these sentences. You may have noticed the patterns but not be aware of the grammar terms. This is absolutely fine: you are a scientist, not a linguist! However, the terms are provided and briefly explained as they are referred to in other parts of the chapter as a form of shorthand, and sometimes as headings. As long as you have a general idea of what they refer to, you should be able to follow the explanations. Some explanations are provided in Chapter 4 and the Appendices.

In 1), the underlined part of the sentence is a **subordinate clause** (a clause which depends on the main clause of a sentence).

▶   **Chapter 4**

The underlined parts of 2), 3) and 4) are **prepositional phrases** (prepositions followed by noun phrases).

▶   **Appendix 1: Noun phrases**

The underlined parts of 5) and 6) are **adverbial phrases** (adverbs and other phrases functioning as adverbs).

The underlined parts of 3), 4), 5) and 6) function as **sentence connectors**, joining two separate sentences together.

All the underlined parts are **adverbials**, i.e. they are used to add information about the situation.

▶   **Chapter 4**

1.1 Prepositional phrases

A prepositional phrase (consisting of one or several words) can occur in different positions, e.g.

- Unusual climatic events have occurred **throughout the year**.
- **Thanks to government funding**, the research is able to continue.

Some common examples of prepositional phrases used in this way in academic writing are those:

- Indicating time, duration or sequence: *in; on; during; throughout; since; until; before; after; prior to*
- Adding information: *in addition to; as well as*
- Indicating exception: *except for; apart from*

- Indicating cause: *because of; as a result of; due to; owing to; thanks to; on account of*
- Indicating concession (allowing for something): *despite; in spite of; notwithstanding*
- Introducing a focus: *with regard to; in terms of*
- Comparing and contrasting: *in comparison with; in contrast to*
- Specifying: *with regard to; with respect to*

■ Practice Task

Choose the correct prepositional phrase.

1) **In spite of/As a result of** measures introduced by the government to limit fuel emissions, pollution has continued to increase.

2) The patients in the study received chemotherapy **in addition to/because of** surgery.

3) **In addition to/Owing to** the risks involved, construction of the tunnel was abandoned.

4) Technology advanced rapidly **throughout/since** the industrial revolution.

5) The government agreed to fund the project, **notwithstanding/apart from** objections put forward by a number of renowned scientists.

1.2 Sentence connectors
Adverbs such as 'however' and phrases such as 'in addition' are often used at the beginning of a sentence to make a connection with the previous sentence. They can also sometimes appear in different positions (note the use of commas), e.g.

- **However**, the outcome was not positive for all patients.
- The outcome was not positive for all patients, **however**.
- The outcome was not, **however**, positive for all patients.

Some common examples of sentence connectors used in academic writing are:

- Sequencing: *firstly; secondly; finally; to begin with; subsequently*
- Adding information: *also; in addition; furthermore; moreover*
- Indicating result: *therefore; consequently; as a result; hence; thus*
- Comparing and contrasting: *similarly; in contrast*
- Indicating concession (allowing for something): *however; nevertheless; nonetheless*
- Emphasising: *in fact; above all; on the contrary*
- Rephrasing: *in other words; that is to say*

1)   'Concession' adverbs like 'however' are very useful for alerting the reader to the fact that things are not as simple or straightforward as they might seem.

2)   Note that the adverbs 'thereby', 'thus' and 'hence' can start a complete sentence or be added to a main clause and followed by *-ing*, e.g.

> The women employ a range of preserving techniques. Thus, they reduce food waste.
> The women employ a range of preserving techniques, **thus** reducing food waste.

■ Practice Task

Choose the correct expression.

1)   The use of antibiotics in farming is increasing. **Consequently/Moreover**, resistance in the general population is decreasing.

2)   The health service in the UK is funded through taxation. **On the contrary/In contrast,** the health service in the USA is based on private insurance.

3)   Flood defences were constructed throughout the region. **However/Therefore**, many parts of the river broke through to flood the land.

4)   Several buildings failed to withstand the earthquake. **In addition/Subsequently**, new building regulations were introduced.

5)   Their data does not support current theories on rising sea levels. **Hence/On the contrary**, it seriously challenges them.

1.3 Controlling syntax

In this section, you will further practise forming the different syntactic structures associated with conjunctions, prepositional phrases and sentence connectors.

■ Practice Task (i)

*Decide which of these are **not** correctly formed.*

1)
   a)   There is a huge amount of soil erosion in the area as a result of the high rainfall.
   b)   There is a huge amount of soil erosion in the area. As a result of the high rainfall.
   c)   Rainfall is high in this area. As a result of this, there is a huge amount of soil erosion.
   d)   Rainfall is high in this area. As a result, there is a huge amount of soil erosion.

2)
    a)   In addition to their many useful built-in functions, smartphones run copious apps.
    b)   In addition to having many useful built-in functions, smartphones run copious apps.
    c)   Smartphones have many useful built-in functions. In addition, they run copious apps.
    d)   In addition their many useful built-in functions, smartphones run copious apps.

3)
    a)   The drug was banned because of its serious adverse side effects.
    b)   The drug was banned because its serious side effects.
    c)   The drug had serious adverse side effects. Because of this, it was banned.
    d)   The drug was banned because there were serious adverse side effects.
    e)   The drug was banned. Because it had serious side effects.

4)
    a)   Asbestos is still widely used in some countries, despite of the serious health risk.
    b)   Asbestos is still widely used in some countries in spite of/despite the serious health risk.
    c)   Asbestos is still widely used in some countries in spite of/despite being a serious health risk.
    d)   Asbestos is a serious health risk. In spite of/Despite this, it is still widely used in some countries.
    e)   Asbestos is still widely used in some countries in spite of/despite the fact that there is a serious health risk.
    f)   Asbestos is still widely used in some countries in spite of/despite there is a serious health risk.

■ Practice Task (ii)

Rewrite the sentences using the expressions given.

1)   After studying computer science for a number of years, he did a PhD in software design.

    subsequently (sentence connector)

    He studied _____

2)   It has been difficult for women to break into the field of science. Despite this, they have been responsible for many important discoveries.

    although (subordinating conjunction)

    Although _____

3)   Although the water subsided quickly after the flood, there was still a huge amount of damage.

    however (sentence connector)

    The water _____

4) The patient was unable to sleep because he was stressed.

    due to (preposition)

    The patient _____

5) Plastics are widely used because they are very versatile. In addition, they are extremely durable.

    in addition to (preposition)

    In addition to _____

6) Some antibacterial products kill bacteria; others only prevent them from multiplying.

    while (conjunction)

    While _____

7) This model of phone is very popular. It has a high degree of functionality.

    owing to (preposition)

    This model of phone _____

> Think about how you could use this technique to produce a simple **paraphrase** of original sources. ▶**Chapter 7**

■ Practice Task (iii)

Join the sentences in as many ways as you can, using the expressions given.

1) The treatment has a high success rate. It has not been adopted on a wide scale.

    despite/in spite of

    _____

    _____

    _____

2) Huge areas of rain forest are being destroyed every day. The number of animal species found in these regions is declining.

    result/because

    _____

    _____

    _____

3) Dyes have many industrial applications. They are also widely used in medicine.

addition

_____

_____

_____

2 Focus on punctuation

Punctuation in English can be viewed as stylistic or grammatical. Stylistic punctuation can involve, for example, deciding between a full stop or a semicolon between two sentences. People have different preferences, and acceptable variation can be found across academic texts. (Style guides will provide information on preferences in certain disciplines or journals ▶Chapter 9.) However, though not governed by 'rules' as such, these choices are still important because they can affect clarity and readability. Grammatical punctuation is not a matter of choice because the punctuation here is intrinsically connected to the meaning, as we saw with relative clauses in Chapter 4.

Focussing on punctuation can help you to consolidate your understanding of sentence structure as a whole. Good command of punctuation can help you achieve clarity and focus in your writing.

■ Explorative Task

Which of the pairs do you find easier to read or more effective? Why? Compare your ideas with the Study Box which follows.

1)
   a) In 1929 Alexander Fleming discovered penicillin.
   b) In 1929, Alexander Fleming discovered penicillin.

2)
   a) St Thomas' hospital concerned about the number of infections began to transfer patients to other centres.
   b) St Thomas' hospital, concerned about the number of infections, began to transfer patients to other centres.

3)
   a) Newton the great mathematician and physicist formulated three laws of motion.
   b) Newton, the great mathematician and physicist, formulated three laws of motion.

4)
   a) The guidelines concerning the prevention of type 2 diabetes recommend plenty of exercise and they propose a diet based around protein, slow-release carbohydrates and fruit and vegetables.

b) The guidelines concerning the prevention of type 2 diabetes recommend plenty of exercise, and they propose a diet based around protein, slow-release carbohydrates, and fruit and vegetables.

5)

a) If detected early enough the disease is treatable.
b) If detected early enough, the disease is treatable.

6)

a) The disease is treatable if detected early enough.
b) The disease is treatable, if detected early enough.

7)

a) Aristotle believed the world to be composed of four elements, earth, water, air and fire.
b) Aristotle believed the world to be composed of four elements: earth, water, air and fire.

8)

a) Mammals are warm-blooded. Reptiles are cold-blooded.
b) Mammals are warm-blooded; reptiles are cold-blooded.

STUDY BOX: COMMON PUNCTUATION PATTERNS

Examples are taken from:

Dawkins, R. (ed.) (2008) *The Oxford Book of Modern Science Writing*.

The **bold** numbers in brackets refer back to the Exploratory Task on punctuation.

▶ **Appendix 3** for information on apostrophes, hyphens, etc.

Also see the next section in Chapter 3 for an explanation of commas, colons and semi-colons in parallel structures.

Commas

"Commas are the equivalent of changing gear when driving; you come to a point where you need to slow down a little or turn a corner. The commas help you negotiate these changes, but also, and perhaps more importantly, they enable you to take your reader along with you."

Peck and Coyle (2012: 54)

Think of commas, therefore, as a way to guide (or drive!) your reader through the text.

1) It can make a sentence easier to follow for the reader if you separate words and phrases coming before (or sometimes after) a clause with a comma (**1**), especially in longer sentences, e.g.

> From Pythagoras to string theory, the desire to comprehend nature has been framed by the Platonic ideal that the world is a reflection of some perfect mathematical form.

The comma serves to 'introduce' the main point, thus guiding the reader.

Likewise, it is often a good idea to use commas if a word or phrase 'interrupts' a clause or structure (**2**), e.g.

> It is mathematics, more than anything else, that is responsible for the obscurity that surrounds the creative process of theoretical physics.

In this way, the reader is able to extract the main point easily.

This principle applies to phrases used in 'apposition', i.e. consecutive phrases, usually noun phrases, the second one defining or modifying the first (**3**), e.g.

> Aristotle, the first great biologist, wrote that each sense organ 'receives the form of the other object without its matter'.

2) It is optional to use an 'Oxford comma' (▶**Chapter 4**) before 'and/but/or' to separate coordinate clauses. However, it can often make a sentence clearer by separating elements and reducing the possibility of ambiguity (**4**). This is often the case with lists, e.g.

> Parallel advances in biochemistry have provided us with detailed knowledge of how energy is converted to chemical bonds and chemical bonds to energy, and how the elementary components of living cells are synthesised.

3) It is common to separate the main clause and subordinate clause with a comma when the subordinate clause comes first (**5**) (▶**Chapter 4**), e.g.

> If we examine the process of DNA replication, we see that there are a number of basic requirements.

If the main clause comes first, it is not necessary to use a comma (**6**), although people often do, and it is considered acceptable if it makes sense. (However, in general, avoid commas which are unnecessary as they can make the page too 'busy' and difficult to read – like driving along a bumpy road!

4) Use commas to separate non-defining relative clauses from the main clause (▶**Chapter 4**), e.g.

> Darwin regarded his work as a clear break with past biology, which believed in an instantaneous creation of an unchanging world whose various parts functioned together like so many parts of a clock.

5) Do not use commas:

  – in defining/restrictive relative clauses (▶**Chapter 4**), e.g.

  > This is the first book, that/which he wrote. ✗

  – to introduce that-clauses (▶**Chapter 4**), e.g.

  > It is thought, that these climatic events will continue. ✗

  – directly in between a subject and verb, no matter how long the subject (▶**Appendix 2**), e.g.

  > The most significant discoveries made in this period, were in the field of space exploration. ✗

Colons and semicolons

1) Use a colon to introduce a sentence that expands in some way on the previous one by, for example, providing an explanation or listing items (**7**), e.g.

> The graph of points for pairs of snapping shrimps always shows a correlation of the sizes of mates: bigger males pair with bigger females, smaller males with smaller females.

2) A semicolon can be used instead of a full stop to separate sentences which are closely connected (**8**), e.g.

> A newborn infant is not a blank page; however, his genes do not seal his fate. Atoms are assembled into complex molecules; these react, via complex pathways in every cell, and indirectly lead to the entire interconnected structure that makes up a tree, an insect or a human.

■ Practice Task

Add commas, colons or semicolons to the following sentences where necessary or so that they are easier to follow. Note that some sentences do not require any further punctuation and it may make them grammatically incorrect.

1) Over the past two centuries pollution has become one of the most pervasive and multi-faceted threats to human health.

2) In 1988 the Centers for Disease Control (CDC) concerned about the spread of HIV in hospitals published a set of universal procedures requiring all medical facilities in the United States to conform to specific guidelines for patient care (Table 6.2).

3) Darwin was concerned with evolution i.e. change over time and he proposed a process natural selection that could bring about such change.

4) Chemical reactions normally occur in water and water can also participate in reactions.

5) If every individual in the world were to demand as much energy as the average person uses in North America the global energy supply industries would require a five-fold increase in their use of primary energy sources.

6) After felling a tree has to be processed in order to render the timber suitable for man's use.

7) The calculus of variations which plays an important role in both pure and applied mathematics dates from the time of Newton.

8) The computers which form the basis of those used today were mainly developed in the 1940s.

9) Scientists are able to identify parts of the brain that are specifically targeted by addictive drugs.

10) Einstein in his general theory of relativity (1915) proposed that the universe exists in four-dimensional space-time.

11) Aromatherapy users showed prominent characteristics they were far more likely to be younger females highly educated who tend to live in urban areas.

12) The pH of the heartwood varies in different species of timber but is generally about 4.5 to 5.5 however in some timbers such as eucalypt oak and western red cedar the pH of the heartwood can be as low as 3.0.

3 Parallel structures

When two or more similar things are mentioned in a sentence, **parallel structures**, that is to say repetition of words, phrases and syntactic patterns (including punctuation), are often employed. Parallel structures are carefully balanced organisational structures based on repetition and contrast. Repetition of certain known or assumed or purely grammatical elements gives focus to new, important or contrasting information.

Some examples follow, with the repeated elements highlighted in bold, and the main contrastive elements underlined:

- Elderly patients are advised to take moderate exercise including walk**ing**, garden**ing** and danc**ing**.
- Ibuprofen **is** primarily **metabolised in the** kidneys; paracetamol **is processed in the** liver.
- There are many reasons for an error in administering medication. Two common types are: procedural **error** (**e.g.** fail**ing** to check the patient's identity) and clinical **error** (**e.g.** administer**ing** the wrong drug or dose).
- Physical medicine has made significant progress in dealing with the consequences of trauma, illness and disease: **it has cured** people of terrible diseases such as smallpox; **it has enabled** people to survive following traumatic injuries; and, through transplantation, **it has extended** the lives of those with failing organs.

The first example is very simple. Three terms are listed with the same grammar, an *ing*-form of the verb:

- walking, gardening and dancing

Parallel structures enhance flow here. And even though the sentence is very simple, it requires a number of important elements: an introduction to the list ('including'), and a conjunction ('and') before the final item in the list. The use of commas is also important, with two possible variations in a simple list like this:

- a, b + c
- a, b, + c

The second choice, with an Oxford comma (►**Chapter 4**), can be helpful in more complex lists.

In the second example, two passive constructions are combined using a semicolon:

- . . . **is metabolised in the** . . .; . . . **is processed in the** . . .

The repetition, including careful repetition of the preposition ('in') and definite article ('the'), give focus to the contrasting information at the end of each clause ('kidneys' vs 'liver'). There is also a clear contrast of degree, with the adverb 'primarily' distinguishing the first clause.

In the third example, a colon is used to introduce and compare two types of clinical error. A colon is a good way to focus the reader on what is coming next, and a good way to introduce two-part or multi-part explanations. The two errors are then described with parallel structures:

- adj + error (e.g. . . . ing . . .) and adj + error (e.g. . . . ing . . .)

Again, the use of repeated terms and structures for what is common to both parts of the explanation helps highlight what it is that differentiates them. Note that the parallelism extends beyond lexis and grammar to the use of 'e.g.' and the use of brackets.

In the fourth example, once again a colon is used to introduce the explanation, but this time it is a three-part explanation and the parts are separated by semicolons. This is a good strategy for more complex listing of items. Each of the three parts starts in the same way, i.e. with 'it' + a verb in the present perfect form:

- It has cured . . .; it has enabled . . .; it has extended . . .

As mentioned earlier, parallel structures are organisational structures based on repetition and contrast. The text changes in small increments, whilst retaining invariant elements. McIntyre calls this "organic change" and "lucid repetition" (1997). As is discussed in Chapter 6, repetition is an important element of cohesion in texts. It has been suggested that its use reduces the amount of processing required by the reader so that they are "freer to attend to the overall message" (Tyler, 1994: 686). By repeating information which is the same, the reader is led to focus on the information which is new or contrasting.

Be careful to avoid 'false parallelism', i.e. when items in a list do not share the same grammar, e.g.

Composite materials are widely used in a variety of applications in, for example, transport, construction, and biomedical. ✗

Composite materials are widely used in a variety of applications in, for example, transport, construction and **biomedicine.** ✓

■ Explorative Task

Find examples of lists and parallel structures in the sentences that follow. What do you notice about punctuation? Compare your ideas to those discussed in the Study Box that follows.

1) Some of the most unusual and versatile of all the mammals are the groups that live, feed and reproduce under water.

2) Epidemic outbreaks of disease are fostered by factors such as poor socioeconomic conditions, ignorance of the cause of infection, natural disasters, and poor hygiene.

3) In actively respiring tissues, where the concentration of carbon dioxide is high, haemoglobin readily releases its oxygen, while in the lungs, where blood carbon dioxide is low, haemoglobin readily binds oxygen.

4) A cancer that arises in epithelium is called a carcinoma; one that arises in connective tissue is called a sarcoma.

5) There are three basic types of water pollutants: toxic chemicals, biological materials and thermal discharges.

6)   Optical astronomical telescopes fall into two main classes: refracting telescopes (or refractors), which use lenses to form the primary image, and reflecting telescopes (or reflectors), which use mirrors.

7)   The cell cycle can be divided into four main stages: the M phase, which consists of mitosis (nuclear division) and cytokinesis (cytoplasmic division); the G_1 phase, in which there is a high rate of biosynthesis and growth; the S phase, in which the DNA content of the cell doubles and the chromosomes replicate; the G_2 phase, during which the final preparations for cell division are made.

STUDY BOX: A SUMMARY OF PUNCTUATION IN PARALLEL STRUCTURES

Numbers in **bold** refer back to the Explorative Task.

1)   Three simple items in a list should be written 'a, b and c' (**1, 2**), though a comma is often used before 'and', and can sometimes aid clarity if the items are long or contain another 'and' within, e.g.

   an equal balance of carbohydrates, fruit and vegetables, and protein

2)   Precise, 'mirrored' (i.e. the same punctuation used in each parallel item), use of commas can enhance the use of parallel structures and improve readability (**3**).

   In actively respiring **tissues, where** the concentration of carbon dioxide is **high, haemoglobin** readily releases its oxygen, while in the **lungs, where** blood carbon dioxide is **low, haemoglobin** readily binds oxygen.

3)   Semicolons can also be used to enhance the link between parallel structures in two separate main clauses (**4**).

4)   A colon can be used to introduce a list (**5, 6, 7**), especially if it is complex. The items in a list can be separated with commas if fairly short and simple (**5, 6**); longer, more complex items can be clearer if separated by semicolons (**7**). This type of structure can be extended to form a whole, single-sentence paragraph, as with (**7**).

■ Practice Task

Combine the following notes to form sentences. Use parallel structures where possible, and commas, colons and semicolons where necessary. You will also need to form the verb correctly, add articles, etc. in order to form grammatical sentences.

1) rock – three types – igneous/sedimentary/metamorphic

2) blood vessels – three types – arteries (carry blood away from heart)/capillaries (connect arteries to veins)/veins (carry blood back to heart)

3) deciduous trees (lose their leaves seasonally)/evergreen trees (green foliage all year round)

4) taste – four types (according to western experts) – sweet/salty/sour/bitter – also umami (according to eastern experts)

5) trunk of a tree – three physical functions to perform – firstly must support crown – region responsible for production of food and seed – secondly must conduct mineral solutions absorbed by roots upwards to crown – thirdly must store manufactured food (carbohydrates) until required

The following reflective and review tasks will help you to consolidate your understanding of Chapter 5.

■ Reflective Task

1) Which expressions and structures from this chapter do you now feel more confident using?

2) Are there any major differences between punctuation use in English and in your first language?

3) Do you currently use parallel structures in your writing? Do you think this is something you might try in future?

■ Review Task

1) Select a text that you have written or are in the process of writing.

2) Try to improve the text by focusing on sentence structure and punctuation.

3) Is there anything in the text which could be expressed effectively with the use of parallel structures?

> In this chapter, we have explored different ways of combining elements in a sentence and building complexity in texts. In the next chapter, we will look at how sentences combine to form bigger units: paragraphs.

Sources of example texts

Dawkins, R. (ed) (2008) *The Oxford book of modern science writing.* Oxford: Oxford University Press, pp 34, 41, 60, 88, 363.

Domone, P. and Illston, J. (eds) (2010) *Construction materials: Their nature and behaviour,* Abingdon: Spon Press, pp 414, 487.

Gregory, J. (2015) Medicines management. In D. Burns (ed.) *Foundations of adult nursing.* London: Sage, pp 89–108, p 95.

McCracken, K. and Phillips, D. (2012) *Global health: An introduction to current and future trends.* Abingdon: Routledge, pp 108, 232.

Oxford Dictionary of Science (2005) Oxford: Oxford University Press, pp 127, 145–146, 805.

Pryjmachuk, S. (2011) Theoretical perspectives in mental health nursing. In S. Pryjmachuk (ed.) *Mental health nursing: An evidence-based introduction.* London: Sage, pp 3–41, p 12.

Yamashita, H., Tsukayama, H. and Sugishita, C. (2002) Popularity of complementary medicine in Japan: A telephone survey. *Complementary Therapies in Medicine,* pp 10, 84–93, p 91.

References

McIntyre, M. (1997) Lucidity and Science I: Writing skills and the pattern perception hypothesis. *Interdisciplinary Science Reviews,* 22, 199–216.

Peck, J. and Coyle, M. (2012) *Write it right: The secrets of effective writing* (2nd edition). New York: Palgrave Macmillan.

Tyler, A. (1994) The role of repetition in perceptions of discourse coherence. *Journal of Pragmatics,* 21, 671–688.

CHAPTER

6

Paragraph development

Achieving flow

This chapter will explore some of the characteristics of English paragraph structure. It will equip you with strategies to help you develop your own paragraphs in a clear way and achieve 'flow' in your writing.

1 Flow

A paragraph should be developed so that there is a logical connection between ideas, and so that the words, sentences and ideas flow in such a way that the reader is able to follow easily. This idea of 'flow' in writing is an important one and there are a number of strategies and cohesive devices which can help you to achieve flow in your own writing.

■ Explorative Task

Look at the student's first and second drafts of a report on a Chemistry MSc Research and Communications module at the University of Manchester. What changes has the student made? Do these make the text easier to read? How?

■ Text A

The dithiocarbamate drug disulfiram is used in the treatment of alcohol abuse. The drug induces apoptosis* in cancer tumours. It has recently been discovered that disulfiram has potential therapeutic capabilities.[1] It has been reported that disulfiram in combination with copper (II) salts causes apoptosis in a chemotherapy-resistant cancer cell line.[2] The copper complex of the drug enhances the result against the tumour cells.

*cell death

DOI: 10.4324/9781003118572-7

■ **Text B**

The dithiocarbamate drug disulfiram is primarily used in the treatment of alcohol abuse. Recently, however, other potential therapeutic capabilities have been discovered.[1] It has been reported that disulfiram causes apoptosis in a chemotherapy-resistant cancer cell line. This effect is enhanced if the drug is used in combination with copper (II) salts.[2]

Text A is the student's first draft. Although accurate and well-expressed on the whole, it is a little hard to follow because the same information is repeated at different points and the writing is not as concise as it could be. Text B is the student's second draft. It flows clearly and concisely from point to point, and uses certain expressions to make meaningful connections:

- 'primarily' clearly contrasts with 'other';
- 'however' alerts the reader to the fact that the situation is more complex;
- 'this effect' makes a clear reference to an effect described in the previous sentence – the writer is then able to give focus to some important new information, something which relates to the main research question.

Textual elements which contribute significantly to flow are:

- information structure
- cohesive devices
- punctuation

These will be discussed in the following sections.

1.1 Information structure
One thing which can aid flow is the structuring of information in a clear, logical way. It is important to be aware of some specific things about English information structure.

1.1.1 Given and new information
The order of information can contribute significantly to how a text flows.

■ **Explorative Task**

1) Look at the following paragraphs and decide which one is easiest to read.

i)

■ **Text A**

Substances that are added to food to maintain or improve the safety, freshness, taste, texture, or appearance of food are known as food additives. Salt (in meats such as bacon or dried fish), sugar (in marmalade), or sulfur dioxide (in wine) are some food additives that have been in use for centuries for preservation.

Many different food additives have been developed over time to meet the needs of food production, as making food on a large scale is very different from making it on a small scale at home. To ensure processed food remains safe and in good condition throughout its journey from factories or industrial kitchens, during transportation to warehouses and shops, and finally to consumers, additives are needed.

■ **Text B**

Substances that are added to food to maintain or improve the safety, freshness, taste, texture, or appearance of food are known as food additives. Some food additives have been in use for centuries for preservation – such as salt (in meats such as bacon or dried fish), sugar (in marmalade), or sulfur dioxide (in wine).

Many different food additives have been developed over time to meet the needs of food production, as making food on a large scale is very different from making them on a small scale at home. Additives are needed to ensure processed food remains safe and in good condition throughout its journey from factories or industrial kitchens, during transportation to warehouses and shops, and finally to consumers.

ii)

■ **Text A**

Geckos, harmless tropical lizards, are extremely fascinating and extraordinary animals. They have very sticky feet that cling to virtually any surface. This characteristic makes it possible for them to rapidly run up vertical walls and along the undersides of horizontal surfaces. In fact, a gecko can support its body mass with a single toe! The secret to this remarkable ability is the presence of an extremely large number of microscopically small hairs on each of their toe pads. When these hairs come into contact with a surface, weak forces of attraction (i.e. van der Waals forces) are established between hair molecules and molecules on the surface. The fact that these hairs are so small and so numerous explains why the gecko grips surfaces so tightly. To release its grip, the gecko simply curls up its toes, and peels the hairs away from the surface.

■ **Text B**

Geckos, harmless tropical lizards, are extremely fascinating and extraordinary animals. They have very sticky feet that cling to virtually any surface. They are able to rapidly run up vertical walls and along the undersides of horizontal surfaces, thanks to this characteristic. In fact, a gecko can support its body mass with a single toe! The presence of an extremely large number of microscopically small hairs on each of their toe pads is the secret to this remarkable ability. Weak forces of attraction (i.e. van der Waals forces) are established between hair molecules and molecules on the surface when these hairs come into contact with a surface. The fact that these hairs are so small and so numerous explains why the gecko grips surfaces so tightly. The gecko simply curls up its toes, and peels the hairs away from the surface to release its grip.

Texts i) B (adapted from WHO) and ii) A (Callister, 2007: 15) are the original texts. Both have a typical English information structure in that each sentence first refers back to the main theme of the previous sentence and then adds new information. This maintains the flow of information. In contrast, in i) A and ii) B, the link to what has gone before is delayed, making the texts difficult to follow.

This **given → new** structure also allows for another common feature of English, **end focus**, whereby new information often comes at the end of the sentence, where it has more prominence.

2) Look back at Texts i) B and ii) A and highlight the words/phrases which link back to information already given.   (The use of such links is further examined later in the chapter.)

■ Practice Task

*Rewrite the second sentence (and the third in 4) of these short texts to reflect the **given → new** structure exemplified earlier. There is more than one option for how to do this, but remember that the first part of the second (or third) sentence should refer back to the first sentence.*

1) Cereals are one of the most important staple foods. Wheat, rye, barley, oats, maize, rice, millet and sorghum are the major cereals of the world.

_____

_____

2) Beer is a fermented alcoholic beverage. Malt and hops are the main ingredients of beer.

_____

_____

3) A ligament is a resilient but flexible band of tissue that holds two or more bones together at a moveable joint. Movement of bones at a joint is restrained by ligaments and therefore they are important in preventing dislocation.

_____

_____

4)   Chalk is a very fine-grained white rock composed of the fossilised skeletal remains of marine plankton and consisting largely of calcium carbonate. Toothpaste and cosmetics use chalk. However, blackboard 'chalk' is not the same thing. It is made from calcium sulphate.

_____

_____

1.1.2 General and specific information

Sentences in a paragraph should be logically ordered, and they often follow a linear **general →
specific** pattern. It is also common to make the first sentence a sort of general 'umbrella' (i.e.
covering the rest of the paragraph) statement, which introduces the main theme of the paragraph: this is often referred to as the **topic sentence**. Subsequent sentences will usually expand in some way on this, by providing support such as explanation or exemplification.

■ Explorative Task

*Look at how the following paragraphs are introduced and developed, and match each sentence
with a description of its function in the paragraph, making particular note of the **topic sentence**
in each.*

■ Text A

Infectious diseases remain a major threat to global animal and human health. Recent examples include the 2002 Foot and Mouth Disease outbreak in the UK, the 2003 global epidemic of SARS and the threat of an influenza pandemic. The control of infectious diseases in animals and humans is a problem that needs to be addressed by scientists, veterinarians, healthcare workers, economists, social scientists and policy makers.

sentence 1	a) **gives** examples
sentence 2	b) **introduces** the threat of infectious diseases
sentence 3	c) **states** the need for problem to be addressed

■ Text B

Unless a patient needing an organ has an identical twin, there will always be immunological differences between the patient and the transplanted organ. These differences are immediately recognised by the recipient's immune system, and, depending on how closely the donor and recipient were matched, cause a reaction intended to destroy the transplanted organ. Consequently, transplant patients are placed on drug regimens designed to lessen the immune response against the organ to prevent rejection. These drugs reduce the chances of rejection by diminishing the patients' *overall* immune capability. However, this causes the patient to be more susceptible to infection.

(Strelkauskas *et al.*, 2010: 106)

sentence 1	a) **states** the problem
sentence 2	b) **explains** the negative side effects of the drugs
sentence 3	c) **introduces** the current solution to the problem (drugs)
sentence 4	d) **explains** how the drugs work
sentence 5	e) **introduces** the issue of immunological differences in organ transplant patients

■ Text C

The *Capsicum* family includes a wide variety of peppers ranging from the large sweet peppers to the fiery chilli peppers. Chilli peppers derive their hotness from capsaicin and dihydrocapsaicin (members of the capsaicinoid family), and restaurants specializing in 'hot' foods owe much to these molecules of nature. They work by interacting with the same receptors in your mouth that sense heat. Excessive amounts of capsaicin are toxic because capsaicin prevents the production of certain neurotransmitters and affects the function of neuroproteins in the brain. At high enough concentrations, capsaicin destroys 'substance P' in the nervous system. This effect has now been harnessed for medical use: 'substance P' is associated with the pain suffered by people with, for example, arthritis and inflammatory bowel disease, and application of a cream containing capsaicin results in pain relief.

(Housecroft and Constable, 2010: 1215)

sentence 1	a) **explains** the source of chilli heat
sentence 2	b) **introduces** the capsicum family
sentence 3	c) **explains** the toxic nature of one 'heat' molecule – capsaicin
sentence 4	d) **gives** examples of medical uses of capsaicin
sentence 5	e) **explains** the effects of capsaicin
sentence 6	f) **explains** how the 'heat' molecules produce heat

Note the verbs in bold (**introduce; state; give; explain**), which show that each sentence has a clear role, or function, in the paragraph. For example, it can be clearly seen from the earlier texts that the role of the **topic sentence** is usually to introduce the main theme of the text. When constructing a paragraph, think about the function of each sentence, i.e. what you want each sentence to *do* in your text.

■ Practice Task

Put the following sentences in order to form well-developed paragraphs. Take care to identify the
topic sentence.

■ Text A

1) _____ 2) _____ 3) _____ 4) _____ 5) _____

a) More efficient fluorescent lighting has since been developed, but suffers from flicker and colour purity issues.

b) They are already used in traffic lights and even in museums to illuminate paintings.

c) Lighting has not changed much since the light bulb was invented by Edison and others close to a hundred years ago.

d) LEDs exhibit tremendous brightness, consume little power, come in different colors, and emit little or no heat.

e) Recently, solid state light-emitting diodes (LEDs) have come on the market and are poised to revolutionise the lighting industry.

(Kuno, 2012: 419–420)

■ Text B

1) _____ 2) _____ 3) _____ 4) _____ 5) _____ 6) _____ 7) _____ 8) _____

a) 'Triggers' external to the climate system, such as changes in the Earth's orbit or a brightening or dimming of the sun, could bring this about; so could internal triggers such as emissions of climate-altering gases into the atmosphere.

b) However, palaeoclimatic records show that large, abrupt changes to the global climate have occurred frequently.

c) Temperature changes of up to 16 degrees Celsius and precipitation doublings, for example, have occurred in periods as short as decades or less (Committee on Abrupt Climate Change, National Research Council, 2002) and might therefore presumably happen again.

d) The majority of climate scientists believe the world is in a period of climate warning and associated environmental change and that this is likely to continue for a long time, with significant impacts on human health around the globe.

e) Projected changes this century, while alarming, are envisaged as relatively gradual, making adaptation to the changes easier than would be the case with larger and more abrupt change.

f)   Such changes occur when a threshold in the climate system is crossed.

g)   This would clearly have enormous impacts on global health futures.

h)   This raises the question of whether human-induced greenhouse gas emissions might ultimately trigger abrupt, larger climate change than is currently predicted.

(McCracken and Phillips, 2012: 287–288)

2 Cohesive devices

There should be logical, meaningful connections between the ideas in a paragraph. These
connections can be indicated through the organisation and grammar of the text, and sometimes by the use of particular words and phrases. Look back at the paragraphs you formed on
lighting and climate change in the previous Practice Task.

How were you able to make logical connections between the sentences?

Did the grammar or particular words/phrases help you to link the sentences/ideas together?

You should notice that there are many ways to indicate logical connections in a text; it is not
just a case of adding lots of 'linking words' like 'however' (although these can help if used with
care and precision).

■ Explorative Task

1)   Look again at the texts from the previous section repeated in the following section. This time,
some examples of cohesion have been highlighted. Consider how these words/phrases help
you to make logical, meaningful connections between the ideas. Find examples of:
   • the use of repetition and synonyms
   • the use of pronouns and other expressions to refer back to what has been said
   • the use of linking expressions

■ Text A

Infectious diseases remain a major threat to global animal and human health. **Recent
examples** (1) include the 2002 Foot and Mouth Disease outbreak in the UK, the 2003
global epidemic of SARS and the threat of an influenza pandemic. The control of **infectious diseases** (2) in animals and humans is a problem that needs to be addressed by scientists, veterinarians, healthcare workers, economists, social scientists and policy makers.

■ Text B

Unless a patient needing an organ has an identical twin, there will always be immunological differences between the patient and the transplanted organ. **These differences** (3)
are immediately recognised by the recipient's immune system, and, depending on how

closely the donor and recipient were matched, cause a reaction intended to destroy the transplanted organ. **Consequently** (4), transplant patients are placed on drug regimens designed to lessen the immune response against the organ to prevent rejection. **These drugs** (5) reduce the chances of rejection by diminishing the patients' *overall* immune capability. **However** (6), this causes the patient to be more susceptible to infection.

■ Text C

The *Capsicum* family includes a wide variety of peppers ranging from the large sweet peppers to the **fiery** (7) chilli peppers. Chilli peppers derive **their** (8) **hotness** (9) from capsaicin and dihydrocapsaicin (members of the capsaicinoid family), and restaurants specializing in 'hot' (10) foods owe much to **these molecules of nature** (11). **They** (12) work by interacting with the same receptors in your mouth **that** (13) sense **heat** (14). Excessive amounts of **capsaicin** (15) are toxic because **capsaicin** (16) prevents the production of certain neurotransmitters and affects the function of neuroproteins in the brain. At high enough concentrations, **capsaicin** (17) destroys 'substance P' in the nervous system. **This effect** (18) has now been harnessed for medical use: 'substance P' is associated with the pain suffered by people with, for example, arthritis and inflammatory bowel disease, and application of a cream containing **capsaicin** (19) results in pain relief.

The earlier paragraphs use a range of cohesive devices to link ideas together. These form part of the *Cohesion in English* framework developed by Halliday and Rugaiya (1976). These cohesive devices are listed here with examples from the texts:

1) Repetition of words and phrases: (2) (15) (16) (17) (19)

2) The use of synonyms: (7) and (10); (9) and (14)

3) The use of 'ellipsis', i.e. when words are left out because they are understood through what has gone before (1)

4) The use of pronouns, including relative pronouns (▶ **Chapter 4**), to refer back to nouns (8) (12) (13)

5) The use of 'this/these' + noun (occasionally 'that/those') to refer back to nouns (3) (5)

6) The use of linking words/phrases (4) (6)

2) Add more examples to the list from the paragraph that follows.

The body can defend itself against infection by using two types of immune response, **the innate** (20) and **the adaptive** (21). **The innate immune response** (22) is available to us when we are born and is nonspecific, where nonspecific means that **this response** (23) can react against any infection or pathogen. **In contrast** (24), **the adaptive immune response** (25) is specific, meaning that it responds against a specific pathogen. **The adaptive immune response** (26) also has the gift of 'memory', **which** (27) allows **it** (28) to remember any pathogen **it** (29) reacted against in the past and to respond quickly and powerfully if **that pathogen** (30) returns.

(Strelkauskas *et al.*, 2010: 325)

STUDY BOX: IMPROVING COHESION

1) When you refer back to a noun mentioned earlier in the text, consider whether you should use a pronoun, for example 'it/them', or whether you need to repeat the word to avoid vagueness or ambiguity. Do not be afraid of some repetition as it often aids clarity and can be used effectively and elegantly (▶ **Chapter 5** on **parallel structures);** this is not the same as redundancy, where words are repeated through a lack of conciseness, or information is repeated because the text does not have a clear, linear structure.

2) If you decide to use a synonym, make sure it really is a synonym. ▶ **Chapter 3**

3) When you refer back to something earlier in the text, think about whether you should use a singular or plural pronoun, e.g. 'it' or 'them'/'this' or 'these'.

4) Use linking words carefully and precisely to add real meaning, and not just to 'decorate' the text.

■ Practice Task (i)

Complete the text, by choosing from the pronouns that follow, so that it is grammatical and makes sense:

it/its
this/that/which

One of the most energetic explosive events known is a supernova. These occur at the end of a star's lifetime, when (1) _____ nuclear fuel is exhausted and (2) _____ is no longer supported by the release of nuclear energy. If the star is particularly massive, then (3) _____ core will collapse and in so doing will release a huge amount of energy. (4) _____ will cause a blast wave (5) _____ ejects the star's envelope into interstellar space. The result of the collapse may be, in some cases, a rapidly rotating neutron star that can be observed many years later as a radio pulsar.

(High Energy Astrophysics Science Archive Research Centre)

■ Practice Task (ii)

Select the best option to complete the text so that it flows easily.

Taking omega-3 fish oils could help to protect against skin cancer, Manchester research-ers have found. (1) **The researchers/They** analysed the effect of taking (2) **omega-3/it** on healthy volunteers and found a regular dose boosted skin immunity to sunlight. (3) **Omega-3/It** also reduced sunlight-induced suppression of the immune system, (4) **it/which** affects the body's ability to fight skin cancer and infection.

Professor Lesley Rhodes, from the Photobiology Unit Dermatology Centre, based at the School of Medicine and Salford Royal NHS Foundation Trust, said: 'Although the changes we found when someone took the oil were small, (5) **it/they** suggest that a con-tinuous low level of chemoprevention from taking (6) **omega-3/it** could reduce the risk of cancer over an individual's lifetime.'

(7) **Professor Lesley Rhodes/She** added that (8) **omega-3/it** was not a substitute for sunscreen and physical protection, but should be regarded as an additional small measure to help protect skin from sun damage.

(*Unilife*, 2013: 10)

■ Practice Task (iii)

Complete the text with a word or phrase from the list so that the connections between ideas are clear.

thus; this knowledge; furthermore; for example; these new materials; these; at this point

The earliest humans had access to only a very limited number of materials, those that occur naturally: stone, wood, clay, skins and so on. With time they discovered tech-niques for producing materials that had properties superior to those of the natural ones; (1) _____ included pottery and various metals. (2) _____, it was discovered that the properties of a material could be altered by heat treatments and by the addition of other substances. (3) _____, materials utilization was totally a selection process that involved deciding from a given, rather limited set of materials the one best suited for an application by virtue of its characteristics. It was not until relatively recent times that scientists came to understand the relationships between the structural elements of mate-rials and their properties. (4) _____, acquired over approximately the past hundred years, has empowered them to fashion, to a large degree, the characteristics of the mate-rials. (5) _____, tens of thousands of different materials have evolved with rather specialized characteristics that meet the needs of our modern and complex society; (6) _____ include metals, plastics, glasses, and fibres. The development of many tech-nologies that make our existence so comfortable has been ultimately associated with the accessibility of suitable materials. An advancement in the understanding of a material type is often the forerunner to the stepwise progression of technology. (7) _____, auto-mobiles would not have been possible without the availability of inexpensive steel or some other comparable substitute. In our contemporary era, sophisticated electronic devices rely on components for what are called semiconducting materials.

(Callister, 2007: 2)

3 Focus on punctuation

As discussed in **Chapter 4** and **Chapter 5,** careful use of punctuation can add significantly to clarity of expression in sentences. It can also greatly improve the flow and readability of a paragraph.

■ Practice Task

Punctuate the following passage so that it flows and makes sense.

an animals survival prospects are greatly improved if the animal alters its behaviour according to its experience learning increases its chances of obtaining food avoiding predators and adjusting to other often unpredictable changes in its environment the importance of learning in the development of behaviour was stressed particularly by us experimental psychologists such as john b watson 1878–1958 and b f skinner 1904–90 who studied animals under carefully controlled laboratory conditions they demonstrated how rats and pigeons could be trained or conditioned by exposing them to stimuli in the form of food rewards or electric shocks this work was criticised by others notably ethologists who preferred to observe animals in their natural surroundings and who stressed the importance of inborn mechanisms such as instinct in behavioural development a synthesis between these two once conflicting approaches has been achieved learning is regarded as a vital aspect of an animals development occurring in response to stimuli in the animals environment but within the constraints set by the animals genes hence young animals are receptive to a wide range of stimuli but are genetically predisposed to respond to those that are more significant

(Oxford Dictionary of Science, 2005: 470)

■ Reflective Task

Look at a paragraph from a piece of writing you recently completed or are working on now and consider the following questions.

1) What do you notice about how it is structured and developed?

2) Is there a topic sentence?

3) Can you find any examples of given-new information structure?

4) Can you find examples of the cohesive devices outlined in this chapter?

5) Does the punctuation help the reader to move easily through the text?

6) Are there any improvements you could make to improve the flow and make the text easier to follow?

■ Review Task

Combine the following notes to form clear, readable paragraphs. Consider:

*   *information structure*
*   *cohesive devices*
*   *punctuation*

(*Remember these are notes: you will need to 'add grammar' – articles, verb forms, etc. – as well as linking together ideas.*)

1) Recycling

recycling products is better than disposing of them as waste – two main reasons:

*   less need to extract raw materials from the earth – conserves natural resources
*   energy requirements for refinement and processing of recycled materials usually less than for natural resources

▶   **Model Text 6, Appendix 4**

2) Additives and chemicals

many foods contain chemical additives – e.g. preservatives; artificial sweeteners; artificial flavourings; colouring agents added by manufacturer during production

chemicals also enter food chain through agriculture:

*   widespread use of fertilisers and pesticides on crops
*   antibiotics and supplements for livestock

maximum allowed levels strictly controlled by law – therefore quality control of raw materials and commercially manufactured foodstuffs essential to ensure they are not contaminated beyond regulatory levels

one technique used: *high-performance liquid chromatography (HPLC)* (technique used to separate, identify and quantify components in a mixture) used in combination with a detection system, often *ultraviolet – visible (UV – VIS) spectroscopy*

▶   **Model Text 7, Appendix 4**

The following reflective and review tasks will help you to consolidate your understanding of **Chapter 6**.

■ Reflective Task

1) Which of the strategies discussed in this chapter do you think will help you most when writing your own paragraphs?

■ Review Task

1) Select a text that you have written or are in the process of writing.

2) Try to improve the text by focusing on paragraph structure.

> In this chapter, we have explored some of the characteristics of English paragraph structure, focusing on how to improve flow. In the next chapter, we will explore how writers make reference to sources.

Sources of examples

Callister, W. (2007) *Materials science and engineering: An introduction*. New York: John Wiley & Sons Ltd.

High Energy Astrophysics Science Archive Research Centre (2015) *Supernova*. Available at: http://heasarc.gsfc.nasa.gov/docs/snr.html (accessed 16th January, 2021).

Housecroft, C. and Constable, E. (2010) *Chemistry: An introduction to organic, inorganic and physical chemistry* (4th edition). Harlow: Pearson Education.

Kuno, M. (2012) *Introductory nanoscience: Physical and chemical concepts*. Abingdon: Garland Science.

McCracken, K. and Phillips, D. (2012) *Global health: An introduction to current and future trends*. Abingdon: Routledge.

Oxford Dictionary of Science (2005) Oxford: Oxford University Press.

Strelkauskas, A., Strelkauskas, J. and Moszyk-Strelkauskas, D. (2010) *Microbiology: A clinical approach*. Abingdon: Garland Science.

Unilife (2013) *The University of Manchester*, 10(6).

WHO (2018) *Food additives*. Available at: www.who.int/news-room/fact-sheets/detail/food-additives (accessed 16th January, 2021).

Reference

Halliday, M. and Rugaiya, H. (1976) *Cohesion in English*. Harlow: Pearson Education.

CHAPTER 7

Referring to sources

This chapter will examine how writers refer to academic sources in an effective way. It will demonstrate how active, purposeful and critical use of sources can help you to build your own argument in assignments. It will outline strategies for effective summary, paraphrase and direct quotation which promote critical engagement with sources, and help you understand how such an approach can help you avoid the risk of plagiarism. It will also provide some ideas on how you might approach synthesising information from multiple sources. Finally, it will suggest ways of repurposing some of the language that you encounter when reading, using it to help express, among other things, your own critical engagement with the literature.

1 Approaching sources actively, purposefully and critically

As discussed in Chapter 2, written assignments often require you to explore a particular topic in depth, usually in response to a particular question or statement, i.e. the assignment task. This is your writing purpose. You will be required to present your own position or viewpoint on the topic. This is often referred to as your **stance**. Your stance emerges through investigation of and critical engagement with the relevant literature. Critical engagement involves analysing, interpreting and evaluating arguments and evidence. You will need to come to some conclusions regarding what you believe to be true, and what arguments and evidence you accept, reject or reserve judgement on.

Your **argument** is a way of organising and expressing your stance. As you express your argument, you will need to summarise, paraphrase and occasionally quote the work of scholars with a clear purpose, i.e. you will need to make it clear why you are referring to a source or sources at a particular point in your writing, while demonstrating how those sources relate to your argument. This is partly how you express your own **voice**, as distinct from other voices (sources) in the text.

DOI: 10.4324/9781003118572-8

Some common criticisms related to source use include:

- A 'patchwork' approach to sources, where a student merely reports what various scholars say, without engaging critically or making it clear how the sources relate to what it is that they themselves want to say;
- Overuse of direct quotation, often related to a 'patchwork' approach;
- A lack of a clear voice in the writing to say something direct and meaningful about the topic and the literature;
- Referencing which is inaccurate, incomplete or inconsistent.

Some of these issues stem from misunderstandings about how writers should use and make reference to sources in academic work. The following Explorative Task presents some comments I have encountered among students which perhaps reflect some of these misunderstandings.

■ Reflective Task

Discuss these comments made by students. How would you reply to these comments?

- "I can use other people's words as long as I give a reference."
- "If I use my own words to explain someone else's work, I don't need to give a reference."
- "I can paraphrase by replacing some words with synonyms."
- "I must change every word in a source I am using."
- "If I have lots of references to other people's work, it won't be *my* work, it won't be original."

> - "I can use other people's words as long as I give a reference."
>
> In theory, yes, as long as you indicate direct quotation with speech marks. But be careful not to overuse direct quotation as it can drown out your own voice. And if it is not explained and integrated into your own argument, it can lead to the creation of the uncritical 'patchwork' effect mentioned earlier.
>
> - "If I use my own words to explain someone else's work, I don't need to give a reference."
>
> You must always acknowledge your source. This is a form of academic courtesy, i.e. acknowledging the contribution of scholars in your field, and providing the reader with the means of locating the studies and ideas that have informed your work. But referencing is not just about fulfilling an obligation. Referencing is in fact a wholly

positive thing: it allows you to position yourself in your field of study, thus bringing credibility to your own argument.

- "I can paraphrase by replacing some words with synonyms."

This approach does not usually reflect true critical engagement with the literature. You should use the literature for a purpose, not just reproduce it in a slightly adapted form.

- "I must change every word in a source I am using."

Again, this suggests reproduction of the essence of the literature rather than purposeful use. Furthermore, as mentioned earlier, you will need to retain a good deal of technical language used across your discipline. This will be further discussed later in the chapter.

- "If I have lots of references to other people's work, it won't be *my* work, it won't be original."

If you form your own stance from critical engagement with the literature, and argue that stance using your own voice, then your work is original.

■ Explorative Task

Look at the following extract from a conference paper co-written by a doctoral researcher at KTH, Stockholm and answer the questions that follow:

1) How do the authors make reference to sources?

2) What is the purpose of this reference to sources at this point in the text?

3) What language indicates this purpose in the text?

Recently, there are been a growing interest from car insurance companies in designing driver behavior classification systems that could eventually be used to relate their costumers' fees to how they drive. As a part of this solution, it is of interest to accurately classify the level of aggressiveness of their customers' recorded trips. Nevertheless, the large number of trips would not allow to identify for each one the type of driving. Consequently, several works such as [4], [7], and [8] have been conducted to solve this problem by an unsupervised learning approach. In the mentioned work, the goal is to find clusters from the recorded trip data which can be characterised by different levels of the aggressiveness without relying on the labels.

(Jaafer *et al.*, 2020)

References to sources are indicated by numbering, a common convention in engineering papers (▶ **Chapter 9**). The authors make it clear that they are referring to particular sources for a reason, connected to their writing purpose.

They introduce a problem in the field:

> **Nevertheless**, the large number of trips **would not allow** to identify for each one the type of driving.

They refer to the literature to indicate that research has attempted to address this issue:

> **Consequently**, several works such as [4], [7], and [8] **have been conducted to solve this problem** by an unsupervised learning approach.

They clarify the particular aim of the research they refer to:

> **In the mentioned work, the goal is to** find clusters from the recorded trip data which can be characterised by different levels of the aggressiveness without relying on the labels.

2 Plagiarism

Plagiarism involves using someone else's words or ideas without acknowledgement. It doesn't take much to understand why this is so unfair and potentially damaging – just imagine how you would feel if someone did this with your words or ideas. So, it is, rightly, an important issue in the academic world and beyond. Plagiarism is one type of academic and professional malpractice and it can have very serious consequences, both in universities and in wider society. Universities have clearly stated policies on academic malpractice, including plagiarism, and strict procedures for dealing with any perceived breaches of their policies. Many will have software such as Turnitin in place to detect plagiarism in written work.

Rather than thinking of plagiarism as merely 'copying', consider Badge and Scott's definition of plagiarism as "uncritical and unacknowledged use of other people's work" (2009). And rather than asking yourself how to 'avoid plagiarism', focus on how to develop an active, critical, purposeful approach to the literature, which, alongside clear referencing, should naturally avert any risk of plagiarism.

Discussions around 'avoiding plagiarism' are often accompanied by instructions to 'use your own words'. In many respects, this is good advice. Using your own language to write about the facts and ideas you encounter in the literature is part of the writing process we discussed in Chapter 2. As you struggle with the process of explaining difficult scientific concepts in your own words, you will get a good idea of just how well you understand them. Moreover, you will need to use your own language in order to demonstrate to the reader/assessor that you understand what you have read and can explain it in a clear way. However, this idea of using your own words is also a little simplistic. Academic writing often involves using the shared language of your discourse community. Positioning yourself within your own scientific discipline involves using a great deal of technical language common to everyone working within that discipline. Also, trying to change this language will often lead to unnatural, unclear expression.

■ Practice Task

Underline the words and expressions which you <u>wouldn't</u> change if you were paraphrasing the following text.

> Renewable energy has been an area of interest to many since the 1973 OPEC oil embargo. The field, however, has since undergone numerous growth-and-bust cycles. It is currently on the upswing, as evidenced by increased funding in the area, and a renewed sense of urgency to move away from fossil fuels. Solar is one facet of renewable energy, with wind and geothermal being others. The underlying motivation is to take advantage of the Sun's abundant energy by converting it into usable forms, much like photosynthesis in plants. What is needed, though, is an active material or system like chlorophyll that can absorb solar radiation and provide efficient charge separation and/or storage.
>
> (Kuno, 2012: 420)

3 Critical engagement with sources

In this section, we will look at some examples of the kinds of sources that students might be required to refer to. We will explore what critical engagement might mean, and what it might look like in terms of words on the page.

■ Explorative Task: reporting research

1) The references have been removed from this introduction to a research article. Where do you think the authors might make reference to other sources to, for example, evidence claims and add credibility?

> Insufficient sleep, defined as inadequate or mistimed sleep, is increasingly recognised as contributing to a wide range of health problems. Multiple epidemiological studies have shown that self-reported short sleep duration (defined in most studies as ≤6 h) is associated with negative health outcomes, such as all-cause mortality, obesity, diabetes, cardio-vascular disease, and impaired vigilance and cognition. Laboratory studies, in which the sleep of

healthy volunteers was restricted, typically to 4 h for 2–6 d, have identified physiological and endocrine variables that may mediate some of these effects, but in general the mechanisms by which insufficient sleep leads to negative health outcomes remain unidentified.

2) Now compare your predictions with the following complete text.

Insufficient sleep, defined as inadequate or mistimed sleep, is increasingly recognised as contributing to a wide range of health problems (1). Multiple epidemiological studies have shown that self-reported short sleep duration (defined in most studies as ≤6 h) is associated with negative health outcomes, such as all-cause mortality (2), obesity (3), diabetes (4), cardio-vascular disease (5), and impaired vigilance and cognition (6). Laboratory studies, in which the sleep of healthy volunteers was restricted, typically to 4 h for 2–6 d, have identified physiological and endocrine variables that may mediate some of these effects (7), but in general the mechanisms by which insufficient sleep leads to negative health outcomes remain unidentified.

(Moller-Levet *et al.*, 2013)

3) Answer the following questions in relation to the text:

   a) How do the writers indicate that they have surveyed the literature on this topic in depth?
   b) How do the writers indicate that they have engaged critically with the literature? (Look at the verbs they use – what do they tell us?)
   c) What part of their analysis of the topic is not referenced?

■ Explorative Task: conveying argument

Read the following text and compare the paraphrases which follow. Which paraphrase conveys the sense of the writer's original argument? How does it do this?

The most obvious differences between different animals are differences of size, but for some reason the zoologists have paid singularly little attention to them. In a large textbook of zoology before me I find no indication that the eagle is larger than the sparrow, or the hippopotamus bigger than the hare, though some grudging admissions are made in the case of the mouse and the whale. But yet it is easy to show that a hare could not be as large as a hippopotamus, or a whale as small as a herring. For every type of animal there is a most convenient size, and a large change in size inevitably carries with it a change of form.

(Haldane, 1928, in Dawkins, 2008: 54)

■ Paraphrase A

Zoologists at that time paid little attention to differences of size. This can be seen from zoology textbooks, which give no indication that the eagle is bigger than the sparrow, or the hippopotamus larger than the hare, though they do mention the mouse and the whale. Yet it is easy to show that a hare could not be as big as a hippopotamus, or a whale as small as a herring. There is a most convenient size for every kind of animal and a large change in size carries with it a change of form.

■ Paraphrase B

In 1928, Haldane noted the lack of attention paid to differences of size in different animals, pointing to the very limited discussion of this issue in the zoology textbooks of the time. He argued that it could be easily demonstrated that each species has 'a most convenient size', and that large differences in size impact on form.

> In B, the historical context of Haldane's views is more clearly signalled and interpreted, and the use of the reporting verbs 'noted', 'pointing to' and 'argued' clearly attributes the ideas to the original source. In A, there is no clear indication that the ideas come from someone other than the person paraphrasing.

■ Practice Task

Read this conclusion to a research article and complete the tasks which follow.

This study shows that neither recipes created by popular television chefs nor ready meals produced by three leading UK supermarket chains meet national or international nutritional standards for a balanced diet. The recipes seemed to be less healthy than the ready meals on several metrics. Maximum nutritional benefit is likely to be derived from home cooking of nutritionally balanced recipes primarily using raw ingredients, rather than relying on ready meals or recipes by television chefs. Further reformulation of ready meals in line with international nutritional guidelines, and collaboration with television chefs to improve the nutritional quality of their recipes, may also help consumers to achieve a balanced diet.

(Howard *et al.*, 2012)

1) If you were paraphrasing these ideas in the text, which of the verbs in bold would you choose to give an accurate interpretation of the sense of the source text?

   a) Howard *et al.* **imply that/demonstrate that** the recipes created by popular TV chefs are poorer in nutritional value than supermarket ready meals.
   b) Howard *et al.* **prove that/conclude that** home cooking using raw ingredients is likely to be the best way to achieve a balanced diet.
   c) Howard *et al.* **note that/indicate that** supermarket meals are actually healthier than the chefs' recipes in some respects.
   d) Howard *et al.* **advocate/point to** collaboration with TV chefs and supermarkets to improve the nutritional quality of their products.

2) Complete the summary so that it reflects the overall argument of the source text.

> Howard *et al.* (2012) a) _____ that TV chef recipes were as poor in nutritional value as b) _____. Whilst c) _____ that the promotion of home cooking with raw ingredients is probably the best way to improve people's diet, they suggest that collaboration with TV chefs and d) _____ to improve the nutritional quality of their products could also have a e) _____ impact.

References to sources can be either 'author focused', with the name of the author in the sentence, e.g.

> Howard et al. (2012) report that the nutritional value of the recipes popularised by TV chefs is at least as poor as that of supermarket ready meals

or 'information focused', with the author's name included in the reference only, e.g.

> It has been reported that the nutritional value of the recipes popularised by TV chefs is at least as poor as that of supermarket ready meals (Howard *et al.*, 2012).

The choice you make between these will depend on how the source relates to your own argument. Information-focussed referencing is common at the start of a scientific research report, when making very general reference to the literature in order to establish a context, e.g.

> The chemistry of metal diynyl and polyynyl complexes is the focus of current intense activity, with potential applications including the construction of one-dimensional molecular wires and metal containing polymers.[1,2]
>
> (Brown *et al.*, 2010: 2253)

> Buildings in the city of Adapazari, Turkey, suffered heavy damage during the 1999 earthquake. Much of the devastation was attributed to the failure of the low plasticity non-plastic silts (Donahue et al. 2007) that had been deposited by the Sakarya River in its almost annual flooding of the plain over the past 7,000 years (Bol et al. 2010).
>
> (Arel and Onalp, 2012: 709)

4 Strategies for paraphrase and summary

When you refer to the work of other scholars, you might use the following techniques:

- **paraphrase**, i.e. explain something with roughly the same amount of detail
- **summary**, i.e. convey the main ideas of a passage, chapter, article or book in fewer words
- **quotation**, i.e. use somebody else's exact words (relatively infrequent in scientific texts, though sometimes useful, especially for precise definitions): ▶ **Chapter 9** for information on incorporating quotation into your writing

If you attempt to paraphrase or summarise with the text in front of you all the time, it can lead to a mechanical 'word changing' approach. Instead, think about using some of the methods outlined in the Study Box.

STUDY BOX: STRATEGIES FOR PARAPHRASE AND SUMMARY

1) Active, purposeful, critical note-taking

Take notes, but make sure you are expressing them and arranging them in a way that reflects your own thought processes. Use the notes to flesh out your own out-line/argument, rather than just listing the thoughts of others. Indicate how different sources relate to each other as well as the assignment topic. Add your own questions or comments to the notes.

2) Synthesis

Create a diagram or table with headings representing the main **themes** you find in the literature, and add facts, comments, points of view or evidence from each source as you read (with references), in your own words as far as possible. Use the diagram/table to synthesise what you have read, and to highlight how sources relate to each other and to your writing task.

3) Free writing

Read a whole section on an idea, theory, method etc. that is relevant to your response, then sit at your computer and attempt to summarise the main points 'freestyle', i.e. quickly, without stopping or consulting the literature. This will allow you to work through your own understanding of what you have read. When you have finished, you can go back to the original to check both your general under-standing, and particular facts and figures.

The first two tasks in this section deal with simple paraphrase techniques relating to straight-forward paraphrase of scientific fact. The last two activities focus more on critical engagement with the literature.

■ Exploratory Task: paraphrasing scientific facts

Look at the original text and the paraphrases, and then complete the table that follows.

■ Original text

Much of chemistry is concerned with chemical reactions. The factors that control whether a reaction will or will not take place fall into two categories: *thermodynamic* and *kinetic*. Thermodynamic concepts relate to the energetics of a system, while kinetics deal with the speed at which a reaction occurs. Observations of reaction kinetics are related to the mechanism of the reaction, and this describes the way in which we believe that the atoms and molecules behave during a reaction.

> C. E. Housecroft and E. C. Constable, *Chemistry: An Introduction to*
> *Organic, Inorganic and Physical Chemistry*, (4th Edition),
> Harlow, Pearson Education, 2010, 339.

■ Paraphrase A

A great deal of chemistry is concerned with chemical reactions. The factors that control if a reaction will or will not take place fall into two classes: *thermodynamic* and *kinetic*. Thermodynamic ideas are related to the energetics of a system, whereas kinetics deal with the speed at which a reaction occurs. Observations of reaction kinetics relate to the reaction's mechanism, the way in which we think that the atoms and molecules behave during a reaction.

■ Paraphrase B

Chemical reactions, and the factors affecting them, are central to chemistry. Whether or not a reaction will occur is determined by *thermodynamics*, which relates to the energetics (the nature of energy in transformation) of a system, and *kinetics*, which relates to the speed of a reaction.

■ Paraphrase C

Chemical reactions, and the factors affecting them, are central to chemistry. Whether or not a reaction will occur is determined by *thermodynamics*, which relates to the energetics (the nature of energy in transformation) of a system, and *kinetics*, which relates to the speed of a reaction.[1]

References

1. C. E. Housecroft and E. C. Constable, *Chemistry: An Introduction to Organic, Inorganic and Physical Chemistry*, (4th Edition), Harlow, Pearson Education, 2010, 339.

Which text	Text A	Text B	Text C
uses different sentence structure and phrasing, just retaining technical terms?			
selects particular information?			
adds some information?			
is clearly referenced?			
is an acceptable paraphrase?			

A has simply adopted a mechanical word-changing approach.

B and C both explain the information they have selected in their own words (and add their own explanation where necessary), but B is still plagiarism, as there is no acknowledgement that the *facts*, if not the actual *words*, have been taken from a textbook.

■ Practice Task: paraphrasing scientific facts

1) Read the text and complete the student's notes which follow.

Nanotechnology is the understanding and control of matter at dimensions of roughly 1 to 100 nanometers, where unique phenomena enable novel applications. Encompassing nanoscale science, engineering and technology, nanotechnology involves imaging, measuring, modelling, and manipulating matter at this length scale.

At the nanoscale, the physical, chemical, and biological properties of materials differ in fundamental and valuable ways from the properties of individual atoms or molecules, or bulk matter. Nanotechnology R&D (research and development) is directed toward understanding and creating improved materials, devices, and systems that exploit these new properties.

One area of nanotechnology R&D is medicine. Medical researchers work at micro- and nanoscales to develop new drug delivery methods, therapeutics and pharmaceuticals. To provide some perspective, the diameter of DNA, our genetic material, is in the 2.5 nanometer range, while red blood cells are approximately 2.5 micrometers.

A nanometer is one billionth of a meter; a sheet of paper is about 100,000 nanometers thick.

(Adapted from Nanotechnology Initiative, What is nanotechnology?)

Student's notes

Definition of nanotechnology:

- 'understanding and 1) _____' of materials at the nanoscale, i.e. at approximately 2) _____ nanometres

- 1 nanometre = one billionth of a 3) _____

- sheer scale understood if we consider the dimensions of a sheet of paper – approximately 100,000 nanometres in 4) _____

Properties of nanomaterials:

- scale determines 5) _____ of materials – at the nanoscale, physical,

- and biological properties of materials differ from those of atoms, molecules and materials in 6) _____

Applications of nanomaterials:

- goal of nanotechnology – exploit these properties and enable 7) _____ applications

- e.g. medicine; new developments at the nanoscale, at the level of 8) _____, diameter of which = approximately 2.5 nanometres – e.g. medicine – researchers working at micro- and nano-scales to develop new drug delivery methods, therapeutics and pharmaceuticals.

2) Now use the notes to write a concise paraphrase.

▶ **Model Text 8, Appendix 4**

■ **Practice Task: reporting research**

1) Paraphrase the following text using some of the following reporting verbs and expressions:

acknowledge; draw attention to the fact that; according to; conclude that; note

Actual global emissions of carbon dioxide (CO_2) reached a new record of 34.5 billion tonnes in 2012. Yet, the increase in global CO_2 emissions for that year slowed down to 1.1%, which was less than half the average annual increase of 2.9% over the last decade. This development signals a shift towards less fossil-fuel-intensive activities, more use of renewable energy and increased energy saving.

(PBL Netherlands Environmental Agency, *Trends in global CO₂ emissions*, 2013)

▶   Model Text 9, Appendix 4

2)   Paraphrase the information without direct reference to the authors.

▶   Model Text 9, Appendix 4

■ Practice Task: conveying argument

Paraphrase the following text using some of the reporting verbs and expressions given here:

> *argue that; emphasise; explain; according to; attach great importance to; make the connection between; underline the significance of*

The principle instrument of the transition from alchemy to chemistry was the balance. The ability to weigh things precisely put into humanity's hands the potential to attach numbers to matter. The significance of the achievement should not go by unremarked, for it is in fact quite extraordinary that meaningful numbers can be attached to air, water, gold, and every other kind of matter. Thus, through the attachment of numbers, the study of matter and the transformations that it can undergo (the current scope of chemistry) was brought into the domain of the physical sciences, where qualitative concepts can be rendered quantitatively and tested rigorously against the theories that surround and illuminate them.

(Atkins, 2013: 2)

▶   Model Text 10, Appendix 4

5 Synthesising information from multiple sources

Usually, you will want to gather information from a range of sources, and synthesise the information and ideas in those sources in order to relate them to your own argument. The following exercise gives you some basic practice in synthesising from multiple sources. The topic has wide social relevance, but it is unlikely to be directly related to your own field of study. For this reason, some of the texts used in the activity are not as academic as the ones you will access for your assignments. However, the activity will allow you to explore some general approaches to synthesising information.

■ Practice Task

You are going to write an introduction to the following essay question:

> *"Are antibiotics a thing of the past?"*

1)   Start by noting down what you already know in the table.

What is an antibiotic?	
How does it work?	
How have antibiotics benefitted society?	
What are the current problems associated with antibiotic use?	
Is there anything else you think might be relevant or would like to find out?	

2)   Now use the table to make notes from the texts that follow.

- Use the information in the texts to form your stance, i.e. your response to the question: the extent to which you agree or disagree with the proposition.
- Select information which is relevant to your response.
- Use your own words, except for technical terms or anything that you think is 'quotable'.
- Distinguish between fact and opinion.
- Indicate any differences of opinion or perspective, including anything which may challenge your stance.
- Note down any questions or comments of your own. (Is anything unclear? Does anything need further explanation or clarification?).
- Add references, indicating where information comes from more than one source.

■   **Text A**

Antibiotics, also known as antibacterials, are types of medications that destroy or slow down the growth of bacteria. The Greek word *anti* means 'against', and the Greek word *bios* means 'life'.

Antibiotics are used to treat infections caused by bacteria. Bacteria are microscopic organisms, some of which may cause illness. The word bacteria is the plural of bacterium.

Such illnesses as syphilis, tuberculosis, salmonella, and some forms of meningitis are caused by bacteria. Some bacteria is harmless, while others are good for us.

(Nordqvist, 2013)

■   **Text B**

Antibiotics are drugs used for treating infections caused by bacteria. Also known as microbial drugs, antibiotics have saved countless lives.

Misuse and overuse of these drugs, however, have contributed to a phenomenon known as antibiotic resistance. This resistance develops when potentially harmful bacteria change in a way that reduces or eliminates the effectiveness of antibiotics.

(U.S. Food and Drug Administration)

■   **Text C**

It is tempting to think that infections are no longer a widespread cause of death and morbidity. In some places and for some groups, this belief is reasonably valid but elsewhere, despite many advances in infection control and treatment, infectious diseases remain a major threat. New antibiotics are being developed for some conditions, but new and some resurgent viral conditions (such as avian and swine flu, SARS, viral encephalitis, and several others) are of course not amenable to antibiotics, and antivirals are rarely very effective. Moreover, certain 'superbugs', such as MRSAs, are emerging in both hospitals and the community, raising the real threat that antibiotic resistance will become ever more common.

(McCracken and Phillips, 2012: 152)

■ Text D

The discovery of penicillin in 1929 and streptomycin in 1943 heralded the age of antibiotics, and, coincidentally, the founding of the American pharmaceutical industry. Within a decade after World War II, a number of important antibiotics were discovered and developed for therapeutic use. They became the foundation for the treatment of infectious disease. This, along with the introduction of better hygiene, led to a dramatic reduction in worldwide morbidity and mortality due to bacterial infections.

The period from 1950 to 1960 was truly the golden age of antibiotic discovery, as one half of the drugs commonly used today were discovered in that period. Unfortunately, the increasing use of antibiotics for human and non-therapeutic animal use (growth promotion) led all too soon to the development of resistant bacterial pathogens. Recognizing the correlation between antibiotic use and resistance development, much of subsequent antibiotic research has been devoted to the discovery and design of new compounds effective against the successive generations of resistant pathogens.

(Davies, 2006: 287)

■ Text E

Britain's most senior medical advisor has warned that the rise in drug-resistant diseases could trigger a national emergency comparable to a catastrophic terrorist attack, pandemic flu or major coastal flooding.

Dame Sally Davies, the chief medical officer, said the threat from infections that are resistant to frontline antibiotics was so serious that the issue should be added to the government's national risk register of civil emergencies.

She described what she called an 'apocalyptic scenario' where people going for simple operations in 20 years' time die of routine infections 'because we have run out of antibiotics'.

(Sample, 2013)

3)   Now use your notes to write your introduction, with references.

▶   **Model Text 11, Appendix 4**

6 Using your reading to build a bank of common structures and phrases

As mentioned earlier in this chapter, using the exact same (non-technical) structures and phrases as the particular source you are using may constitute plagiarism. However, as you read the literature of your subject, you should try to become aware of common structures and phrases that you could use in the rest of your writing to help you express yourself in a natural way. These can help you to organise your work and develop a critical voice, among other things.

■ Explorative Task

Look back at the texts on antibiotics and pick out any structures and phrases that could be easily used in other contexts.

■ Practice Task

Here you are presented with a structure or phrase from one of the antibiotics texts, and an example of how that structure could be adapted to another context. Add an example based on your own area of study.

1) **the correlation between** antibiotic use **and** resistance development

   • **the correlation between** drug use **and** hepatitis

   _____

2) **Despite many advances in** infection control and treatment, infectious diseases **remain a major threat**.

   • **Despite many advances in** computer science, viruses **remain a major threat**.

   _____

3) This, along with the introduction of better hygiene, **led to a dramatic reduction in** worldwide morbidity and mortality due to bacterial infections.

   • Advances in materials design **led to a dramatic reduction in** fatal car accidents.

   _____

4) **Much of subsequent** antibiotic **research has been devoted to** the discovery and design of new compounds effective against the successive generations of resistant pathogens.

   • **Much of subsequent** cancer **research has been devoted to** the development of vaccines.

   _____

5) **The rise in** drug-resistant diseases **could trigger** a national emergency comparable to a catastrophic terrorist attack, pandemic flu or major coastal flooding.

   • **The rise in** obesity **could trigger** a healthcare crisis.

6) Misuse and overuse of these drugs, however, have **contributed to a phenomenon known as** antibiotic resistance.

   • The adoption of cloud computing has **contributed to a phenomenon known as** 'information sprawl', in which large volumes of data are hosted outside traditional data centres.

See Academic Phrasebank: a useful collection of common structures and phrases taken from a wide range of academic texts.

The following reflective and review tasks will help you to consolidate your understanding of Chapter 7.

■ Reflective Task

1) Have your views on source use and referencing changed in any way as a result of reading this chapter?

2) What do you think you might do differently in future?

■ Review Task

1) Select a text that you have written or are in the process of writing which makes reference to sources.

2) Try to improve the text with reference to the guidance in this chapter.

In this chapter, we have looked at how to use sources in an effective way to build your own arguments. In the next chapter, we will look more into the idea of building an argument, one which is clearly developed and coherent. Chapter 9 provides information on the mechanics of referencing in texts.

Sources of example texts

Arel, E. and Önalp, A. (2012) Geotechnical properties of Adapazari silt. *Bulletin of Engineering Geology and the Environment*, 71, 709–720.

Atkins, P. (2013) *What is chemistry?* Oxford: Oxford University Press.

Brown, N., Collison, D., Edge, R., Fitzgerald, E., Low, P., Helliwell, M., Ta, Y. and Whiteley, M. (2010) Metal-stabilised diynyl radicals. *Chemical Communications*, 46, 2253–2255.

Davies, J. (2006) Where have all the antibiotics gone? *Canadian Journal of Infectious Diseases and Medical Microbiology*, 17(5), 287–290.

Dawkins, R. (ed.) (2008) *The Oxford book of modern science writing*. Oxford: Oxford University Press.

Housecroft, C. and Constable, E. (2010) *Chemistry: An introduction to organic, inorganic and physical chemistry* (4th edition). Harlow: Pearson Education.

Howard, S., Adams, J. and White, M. (2012) Nutritional content of supermarket ready meals and recipes by television chefs in the United Kingdom: Cross sectional study. *BMJ 2012*, 345, e7607.

Jaafer, A., Nilsson G. and Como, G. (2020) Data augmentation of IMU signals and evaluation via a semi-supervised classification of driving behavior, Cornell University. *arXiv:2006.09267*.

Kuno, M. (2012) *Introductory nanoscience: Physical and chemical concepts.* Abingdon: Garland Science.

McCracken, K. and Phillips, D. (2012) *Global health: An introduction to current and future trends.* Abingdon: Routledge.

Moller-Levet, C., Archer, S., Bucca, G., Laing, E., Slak, A., Kabiljo, R., Lo, J., Santhi, N., Schantz, M., Smith, C. and Dijk, D. (2013) Effects of insufficient sleep on circadian rhythmicity and expression amplitude of the human blood transcriptome. *Proceedings of the National Academy of Sciences of the United States of America*. Available at: www.pnas.org/content/110/12/e1132 (accessed 28th February, 2021).

Nanotechnology Initiative. *What is nanotechnology?* Available at: www.nano.gov/html/facts/whatisnano.html (accessed 15th January, 2014).

Nordqvist, C. (2013) What are antibiotics? How do antibiotics work? In *Medical News Today*. Available at: www.medicalnewstoday.com/articles/10278.php (accessed 15th January, 2014).

PBL Netherlands Environmental Assessment Agency (2013) *Trends in global CO2 emissions: 2013 report*. Available at: www.pbl.nl/en/publications/trends-in-global-co2-emissions-2013-report (accessed 15th January, 2014).

Sample, I. (2013) Antibiotic-resistant diseases pose 'apocalyptic' threat, top expert says. In *The Guardian*, 23rd January. Available at: www.theguardian.com/society/2013/jan/23/antibiotic-resistant-diseases-apocalyptic-threat (accessed 15th January, 2014).

U.S. Food and Drug Administration. *Combating antibiotic resistance*. Available at: www.fda.gov/downloads/ForConsumers/ConsumerUpdates/UCM143470.pdf (accessed 2nd December, 2013).

References

Academic Phrasebank. Available at: www.phrasebank.manchester.ac.uk/ (accessed 18th January, 2021).

Badge, J. and Scott, J. (2009) Dealing with plagiarism in the digital age. *Higher Education Academy EvidenceNet*. Available at: http://evidencenet.pbworks.com/w/page/19383480/Dealing%20with%20plagiarism%20in%20the%20digital%20age (accessed 18th January, 2021).

Writing coherent texts and arguments

This chapter will look at how to develop texts and arguments so that they are coherent and easy to follow for the reader. It will analyse a range of scientific texts to investigate how scientific writers structure their texts, and how they organise, sustain and support their ideas. It will examine how writers develop coherent arguments with a clear line of reasoning, and clear critical engagement with sources and ideas. It will also explore useful language for writing definitions.

1 Coherence

Good writing is clear and 'coherent'. This means that it makes sense to the reader. The reader is able to navigate the text easily and follow the ideas. They are able to extract the writer's argument and make sense of it.

The tasks in this chapter enable you to analyse examples of scientific writing in books and journals, as well as examples of student writing, in order to explore certain language and discourse features which can help writers to produce coherent texts and arguments.

2 Text structure

Every text and argument is unique. A writer should develop a text according to their purpose and audience, as discussed in Chapter 1 and Chapter 2. They will select content which is relevant to their purpose and organise it in a way which helps them achieve that purpose and meet the needs of the reader.

2.1 A simple text structure

A text such as an essay, report or review may have a simple structure:

*   Introduction
*   Main body
*   Conclusion

DOI: 10.4324/9781003118572-9

Even with this relatively simple structure, there needs to be careful alignment between the different sections if the text is to be coherent. This can be partly achieved if:

- Text organisation is clearly outlined in the introduction, and aligns with a list of contents, if provided;
- Statements of purpose and rationale are repeated in the introduction and conclusion;
- Terminology is defined in the introduction and then used consistently throughout the text.

■ Exploratory Task

You are going to look at the beginning of a technical report written by a pre-sessional student at the University of Manchester.

1) Read the introduction to the report and use it to help you complete the list of contents which precedes it, using the following headings and sub-headings:
   - The effects of surface treatments and coatings
   - The mechanism of fatigue
   - Final fracture
   - Surface roughness
   - Fatigue crack propagation

An examination of the role of different types of coating in the prevention of fatigue in carbon steel

Contents

1 Introduction

2 _____

    2.1 Fatigue crack initiation

    2.2 _____

    2.3 _____

3 Source and prevention of fatigue

    3.1 _____

    3.2 Residual stresses

    3.3 _____

4 Conclusion

5 References

■ Introduction

Fatigue, the tendency of a material, such as metal, to break after being subjected to cyclic loading, has been the subject of research for more than 150 years. It was Wohler who first discovered that metallic parts could continue to work for a long time if they were subjected to a *constant* load below their yield point, but that parts could fail if they were subjected to a *cyclic* load, even if it was below the yield point of the material [1]. Over the course of the 20th century, many fatigue failures were recorded. However, fatigue was considered to be a puzzling phenomenon because the damage could not be seen, and the only indicator of the problem was a hidden crack. A complete solution to the problem of fatigue has not yet been discovered [1].

The process of fatigue failure can be divided into three stages: crack initiation, crack propagation, and then rapid fracture, which leads to failure [2]. The fatigue crack is more likely to initiate at the surface of the material because of surface roughness or marks left during the manufacturing process. These act as stress concentration points. Therefore, surface treatment, such as surface polishing, is very important to prevent or delay fatigue failure [3]. In addition, metals exposed to corrosive environments may also be treated with coatings, which may affect fatigue behaviour.

The objective of this project is to assess the role of different types of coating in combatting fatigue failure in carbon steel. It will begin by outlining the mechanism of fatigue. It will then discuss the source of fatigue, and ways of preventing it, with particular focus on the use of different coatings.

---

2) Highlight the parts of the text which contain:
   - an opening statement
   - background/context
   - definitions of key terms
   - the rationale behind the investigation
   - the purpose of the project
   - an outline of the project structure

3) How do the parts of the text that you highlighted add to the coherence of the text?

4) Is there anything that would improve the coherence of the text, in your opinion?

2.2 The IMRAD structure

A typical structure in scientific research reports is the IMRAD structure. This stands for:

- **Introduction**

   This introduces the topic and any important background information. It sets the scene and attracts interest. It presents a review of the relevant literature and identifies a gap or problem which forms the basis of a research question. The introduction often contains definitions of key terms.

- **Method**

   This describes the type of study being conducted (quantitative, qualitative, mixed), and the methods of data collection and analysis (e.g. a survey, statistical analysis). This section also covers any ethical considerations.

- **Results**

   This details the findings of the study; tables and figures are often used in this section.

- **Discussion**

   This is where the writer interprets their findings and discusses their meaning and significance. This involves relating findings to current knowledge in the field, and highlighting any new insights or understanding.

Many of the scientific papers that you will read in journals will follow this structure, or something very similar. There may be variations: some may include slightly different headings such as 'Background', 'Related work' or 'Conclusion'; some may combine 'Results' and 'Discussion' sections. Papers will also be preceded by an 'Abstract', summarising the paper.

There are two main reasons why you should familiarise yourself with the IMRAD structure, one connected to reading, one connected to writing. In terms of reading, familiarity with the IMRAD structure will help you to read scientific papers more easily and effectively. You can use the headings to help you navigate papers and find the parts you want to focus on. In terms of writing, the IMRAD structure may form the basis of writing assignments that are based on your own research. Most undergraduate and Master's students write a long research dissertation at the end of their degree, for example. Furthermore, closer inspection of these texts will reveal that there are particular language and discourse features associated with each part of the IMRAD framework. A significant amount of research has gone into investigating these language and discourse features (Swales, 1990), and it has been established that they help writers to perform certain functions in academic writing. The Academic Phrasebank, developed at the University of Manchester by John Morley, is an online resource which can help you explore the language associated with these functions.

In this chapter, we will analyse a range of scientific texts to discern how the use of particular language and discourse features corresponds to coherence in texts and arguments. The following Explorative Task will guide you towards an understanding of some typical language and discourse features associated with the IMRAD structure. The text under analysis has been chosen because it exemplifies some of these language and discourse features, and also because it illustrates how difficult scientific concepts can be explained in a reader-friendly way. So, although the topic may not be directly connected to your studies, you should be able to follow a general thread of reasoning through the text.

■ Explorative Task

You are going to read some extracts from a research paper in a journal of chemical engineering entitled:

Characteristics of Activated Carbons Derived from Deoiled Rice Bran Residues
(Niticharoenwong *et al.*, 2013)

The first exercise will help you with some of the technical vocabulary. Box A deals with fairly common scientific words. Box B deals with the more technical terms connected to this research.

1) Before you read, match these words from the text with their definitions (using a dictionary where necessary):

■ A

i	application	a	soak something with a substance
ii	raw material	b	the total area of an object's surface
iii	surface area	c	a basic material from which other things are made
iv	impregnate	d	the practical use of a material, technology, etc.
v	grind	e	something that is produced when you are making something else
vi	by-product	f	existing in large amounts
vii	abundant	g	make a substance into a powder using a hard surface

■ B

i	pore	a	a substance used to increase the rate of a chemical reaction
ii	activated carbon	b	one of many small openings on a solid substance
iii	leach	c	extract soluble components from a solid using a solvent (a liquid that dissolves a substance)
iv	catalyst		
v	residue	d	carbon that has been processed so that it is full of small pores that increase the surface area available for adsorption or chemical reactions
vi	bran		
		e	the protective layer surrounding a cereal seed
		f	something that remains after a substance has been removed

2) Match the following extracts from the research paper to the following sections. Focus on the language in bold to help you:

Abstract; Introduction; Materials and Methods; Results and Discussion; Conclusion

■ A

First, deoiled rice **was treated with** concentrated sulphuric acid (weight ratio of 1:1), at 150°C for 24 h. **After cooling,** the material **was ground.** The excess acid present on the material **was leached out by washing with** sodium bicarbonate solution (1% w/v) until neutral. The resulting material **was then washed with** distilled water. **After drying at 110°C for 24 h,** the treated material **was impregnated with** H_2PO_4 or $ZnCl_2$. at 1:1 (w/w), and **then dried at 110°C for** another 24 h.

■ B

The research focuses on investigation of the characteristics of activated carbons derived from deoiled bran residues, a major by-product of the rice bran oil industry. **The preparation of** activated carbon **consists of two steps; the first step is** the pre-car-bonised acid leaching (H_2SO_4) process and **the second step is** chemical activation **using** H_2PO_4 or $ZnCl_2$ as an activating agent **for the development of** micropores. **The effects of** preparation parameters **including** the types of activating agent (H_2PO_4 and $ZnCl_2$) and temperature of activation **were studied**.

■ C

Activated carbon **is a well-known material with various applications** on an industrial scale. **For example, it is used for** the purification of gases (Guo and Lua, 2002), the removal of organic pollutants from water (Zhou et al., 2009), the removal of heavy metal from wastewater (Daifullah et al., 2003; Montanher et al., 2005; Singh et al., 2005), and as a catalyst or catalyst support (Bedia et al., 2010; Gu et al., 2010). Activated carbons that are currently commercially available are expensive, **however. Therefore,** the search for alternative low-cost bio-based materials, as well as the appropriate processes for the preparation of activated carbons from these abundant resources, **has become necessary** (Guo and Lua, 2002; Maite et al., 2007).

■ D

Table III shows the BET surface areas of activated carbons **prepared from** H_2PO_4 and $ZnCl_2$ activation **observed at** different activation temperatures. For H_2PO_4 activation, the BET surface area **slightly increases when** the activation temperature increases from 400° to 700°C. **This was possibly because of** a violent gasification reaction **that may cause** a part of the micropore structure to be destroyed by pores collapsing or combining (Oh and Park, 2002)

■ E

This study reports the preparation of activated carbon from deoiled rice bran residues **using** H_2PO_4 and $ZnCl_2$ as chemical activating agents. $ZnCl_2$ activation **produces** an acti-vated carbon with higher surface area than H_2PO_4 produces. The maximum surface area of 1404 m^2/g **was obtained** for $ZnCl_2$ activation at the activation temperature of 400°

C, **while** the maximum surface area of the material activated with H_2PO_4 **was** 1187 m²/g **obtained** at the activation temperature of 500°C. Both H_2PO_4 – and $ZnCl_2$-activated carbons **were found to** exhibit a combination of mostly microporous and partly mesoporous structures. **The results from this study demonstrated that** deoiled rice bran residues **can be** a promising abundant, low-cost material for the preparation of activated carbons. These activated carbons **can be used as** catalyst supports **due to** their remarkably high surface areas.

The following questions will help you to explore some common language features of the different parts of an IMRAD text.

3) Which extracts use a) the present tense b) the past tense?

4) What do you notice about the <u>verbs</u> in the Materials and Methods section?

5) Underline the expressions in the Materials and Methods section which <u>indicate sequence</u>.

6) Which expressions in the Results and Discussion section:
   • <u>refer directly to results/data</u>
   • <u>discuss results</u>

7) Which phrase in the Conclusion <u>introduces a summary of results</u>?

8) Underline words in the Conclusion which <u>indicate similarities and differences</u> in the results for the two methods?

9) What is the function of the last two sentences in the Introduction and Conclusion?

10) Highlight all the <u>precise measurements</u> provided. Why do the authors include these at particular points in the text?

▶   **Chapter 9** for more information on presenting measurements in science

Note how consistent tense use, clear sequencing and the use of organisational language make the texts easy to follow, despite the complexity of the science.

3 Building a coherent argument

In academic writing, an argument is the organisation and expression of the writer's stance. For an argument to be coherent, it must have a clear line of reasoning, developed through critical engagement with relevant literature and supported by evidence. An argument is usually built through a series of steps, each one preparing the ground for the next one. The following Explorative Tasks explore some of the steps writers take as they build their arguments. The first task looks at how writers begin their arguments to lay the groundwork for further discussion. The second task looks at several steps in the introduction of an argument.

■ Explorative Task (i)

■ Text A

Read the passage and complete the table which follows, highlighting any particular language which helps you.

Owing to its enormous body mass, the small surface-to-volume ratio and the lack of sweat glands (Spearman, 1970; Hiley, 1975; Wright, 1984; Mariappa, 1986), elephants are confronted with unusual problems concerning heat dissipation and drying of the integument (Lillywhite and Stein, 1987). Control of skin temperature is an extremely important mechanism in elephants' temperature regulation (Phillips and Heath, 1995) and the most important thermoregulatory organs to use this pathway are the elephants' ears. The ears of the African elephant have a large surface-to-volume ratio as well as an extensive and prominent vascular supply, which predestines these organs for optimal heat dissipation (Wright, 1984).

(Weissenbock *et al.*, 2010: 182)

Claims	Cause/Reason	Source
Elephants find it difficult to keep cool.		
The ears of an elephant are the most important organ for regulating its temperature.		

■ Text B

Read the passage and complete the table which follows, highlighting any particular language which helps you.

Overweight and obesity are major threats to public health globally. One estimate suggests that 1.46 billion adults worldwide were overweight in 2008,[1] and projections suggest that by 2020 over 70% of adults in the United Kingdom and United States will be overweight.[2] This is likely to result in millions of additional cases of diabetes and heart disease and thousands of additional cases of cancer.[2]

References

1. Finucane MM, Stevens GA, Cowan MJ, Danaei G, Lin JK, Paciorek CJ, et al. National, regional, and global trends in body-mass index since 1980: systematic analysis of health examination surveys and epidemiological studies with 960 country-years and 9·1 million participants. Lancet 2011; 377:557–67.

2. Wang YC, McPherson K, Marsh T, Gortmaker SL, Brown M. Health and economic burden of the projected obesity trends in the USA and the UK. Lancet 2011;378:815–25.

(Howard *et al.*, 2012)

Statement	Premise (assumed fact behind the claim)	Support (statistical evidence for the premise)	Source
Overweight and obesity are major threats to public health globally.	Large numbers of people are over-weight/obese.		

■ Explorative Task (ii)

Look at the first part of the introduction from the article we analysed earlier in this chapter

Characteristics of Activated Carbons Derived from Deoiled Rice Bran Residues

(Niticharoenwong *et al.*, 2013)

and answer the questions which follow.

■ Introduction

Activated carbon is a well-known material with various applications on an industrial scale. For example, it is used for the purification of gases (Guo and Lua, 2002), the removal of organic pollutants from water (Zhou et al., 2009), the removal of heavy metal from wastewater (Daifullah et al., 2003; Montanher et al., 2005; Singh et al., 2005), and as a catalyst or catalyst support (Bedia et al., 2010; Gu et al., 2010). Activated carbons that are currently commercially available are expensive, however. Therefore, the search for alternative low-cost bio-based materials, as well as the appropriate processes for the preparation of activated carbons from these abundant resources, has become necessary (Guo and Lua, 2002; Maite et al., 2007).

In principle, the methods for preparing the activated carbons can be divided into two categories: physical activation and chemical activation (Ahmadpour and Do, 1996). In physical activation, a raw material is first carbonized and the carbonized material is then activated by steam (Li et al., 2008), carbon dioxide (Guo et al., 2009), air (Su et al., 2006), or their mixture. In chemical activation, a raw material is impregnated with an activation agent such as an acid while being heat-treated under inert atmosphere (Basta et al., 2009; Guo et al., 2002; Liou and Wu, 2009). Often combinations of chemical activation followed by physical activation methods are employed to improve the characteristics of activated carbon, such as surface area and pore volume (Azevedo et al., 2007). It has been widely accepted that activated carbons prepared using different types of raw materials, activation processes, types of precursors, or compositions and process conditions result in different textural and functional characteristics. For example, activated carbons derived from coconut shell with air activation have a surface area of 700 m^2/g (Su et al., 2006), while steam activation gives a maximum surface area of 1,962 m^2/g (Li et al., 2008), CO_2 activation gives a maximum surface area of 1700 m^2/g (Guo et al., 2009), and chemical activation with $ZnCl_2$ followed by physical activation gives a maximum surface area of 2,114 m^2/g (Azevedo et al., 2007).

Thailand is the sixth largest rice producer in the world . . .

1) In the first paragraph, how do the writers:
   a) Establish the importance of the topic?
   b) Draw attention to a current problem?
   c) State the need for a solution?
   d) Prepare the ground for a discussion of the role of rice as a potential solution to the problem?

2) Which phrases link the first and second paragraphs?

3) In the second paragraph:
   a) How many separate points are covered?
   b) Which phrases and punctuation help to organise the points?

4) How do you expect the third paragraph to continue? How do the preceding paragraphs prepare for this?

5) Complete the following sentence to describe the argument that the authors develop in the paper as a whole:

> The characteristics of activated carbons derived from deoiled rice bran residues make rice a p_____ raw material for the p_____ of activated carbon.

6) Match the following sentence halves to summarise the reasoning behind the argument.

a)	Activated carbon is a useful material,	(i)	we need to find ways of lowering the cost of production.
b)	**As** it is expensive to produce,	(ii)	**Therefore**, if it turns out to be suitable for the production of deactivated carbon, there will be a plentiful supply of raw material.
c)	Using low-cost bio-based materials would help reduce the cost of production,		
d)	Different processes work differently with different materials, affecting the characteristics of the finished product.	(iii)	**so** rice, as a relatively cheap biological product, might be a good alternative.
		(iv)	**so** we need to produce more of it.
e)	Rice is abundant in Thailand.	(v)	**For this reason**, it will be interesting to see how rice reacts.

7) How do the authors support their reasoning to produce a credible argument?

4 Focus on the language of methods, results and discussions

There are some typical language patterns which occur in these sections of a paper.

As discussed in previous tasks in this chapter, methods sections are often characterised by past simple and passive verb forms, together with sequence markers. Certain typical prepositional use can also be commonly found.

■ Practice Task

1) Complete the text from the Methodology section of a paper with the correct form of the following verbs, taking care to consider which of them need to be passive:

focus; spend; have; release; feed; observe

The observations via infrared thermography a) _____ on the elephant group at the Vienna Zoo, Austria. T_s (skin temperature) of four adult female elephants and two juvenile elephants b) _____. The keepers c) _____ direct contact with the group for approximately 1.5 h per day. The elephants d) _____ the night unchained in the indoor enclosure within the family and e) _____ to their outdoor enclosure for approximately 4 h during the day. The elephants f) _____ with hay, branches, carrots and apples.

(Weissenbock *et al.*, 2010: 182)

2) Complete the sentences with the correct preposition.

    a) The solution was heated _____ 150°C.
    b) The environment was kept _____ a steady temperature _____ 18°C.
    c) The glass was treated _____ corrosive acids to produce a matte finish.
    d) The elephants were enclosed _____ 1pm and 4pm.
    e) The patients attended physical therapy from 11am _____ 1pm each day.

3) Put the words in order to make sentences describing methodology.

   a) material/the/cut/was/into/strips/2 cm

   _____

   b) the/cooling/was/mixed/after/solution/with/10 ml/water/of

   _____

   c) months/the/installed/system/was/alarm/throughout/the/and/building/then/
      monitored/six/for

   _____

   d) corrosion/to/prevent/metal/the/was/with/a/coating/treated

   _____

   e) conducted/post-natal/were/using/surveys/email/groups/and/focus

   _____

**STUDY BOX: COMMON STRUCTURES
IN METHODS SECTIONS**

To do x, y was done

Y was done to do x

X was done (by) using y

After/Before____ing, x was done

Prior to x, y was done

Describing and discussing results can involve a range of descriptive and analytical language.

■ Practice Task

You are going to look at extracts from a paper entitled:

Nutritional quality of organic foods: a systematic review

(Dangour _et al._, 2009)

1) Complete these sentences from the results and discussions sections of this paper with the phrases provided:

several strengths; were significantly higher (x 2); beyond the scope of; found no evidence of; it is unlikely that; are comparable; there is no evidence to support

Results

a)   Analysis of satisfactory-quality crop studies _____ a difference in 8 of the 11 nutrient categories.

b)   Nitrogen contents _____ in conventionally produced crops, and contents of phosphorus and titratable acidity _____ in organically produced crops.

Discussion

c)   The analysis presented suggests that organically and conventionally produced foods _____ in their nutrient content.

d)   _____ consumption of these nutrients at the concentrations reported in organic foods in this study provide any health benefit.

e)   This review had _____, such as its systematic and exhaustive nature, its broad inclusion criteria, and its methodological rigor.

f)   The potential for any benefits to public health [. . .] warrant further systematic review, but [this] was _____ the current report.

g)   One broad conclusion to draw from this review is that _____ the selection of organically produced foodstuffs over conventionally produced foodstuffs to increase the intake of specific nutrients or nutritionally relevant substances.

2) Which of the earlier sentences make reference to the following?
   * specific findings based on data
   * general findings
   * the implications of the findings
   * the strengths of the study
   * limitations of the study
   * the need for further research

5 A simple strategy using repetition to maintain coherence through a text

One strategy that can help achieve coherence in a text is repetition. As we saw in Chapter 5 and Chapter 6, repetition is an important cohesive device. There are simple strategies based around repetition which can hold a long text together, and thus help the reader navigate easily.

■ Explorative Task

1) What do you understand by the term 'masonry'?

2) Read the text on masonry and complete the table which follows from the following list:

history; definition; main techniques; technical analysis on a key point; basic principle

■ Paragraph 1

Over the last three decades the term 'masonry' has been widened from its traditional meaning of structures built of natural stone to encompass all structures produced by stacking, piling or bonding together discrete chunks of rock, fired clay, concrete, etc., to form the whole. 'Masonry' in this wider sense is what these chapters are about. In contemporary construction most masonry in the UK is built from man-made materials such as bricks and blocks. Stone, because of its relatively high cost and the environmental disadvantages of quarrying, is mainly used as a thin veneer cladding or in conservation work on listed buildings and monuments.

■ Paragraph 2

Second to wood, masonry is probably the oldest building material used by man; it certainly dates from the ancient civilisations of the Middle East and was used widely by the Greeks and Romans. Early cultures used mud building bricks, and very little of their work has survived, but stone structures such as the Egyptian pyramids, Greek temples and many structures made from fired clay bricks have survived for thousands of years. The Romans used both fired clay bricks and hydraulic (lime/pozzolana) mortar and spread this technology over most of Europe.

■ Paragraph 3

The basic principle of masonry is of building stable bonded (interlocked) stacks of handleable pieces. The pieces are usually chosen or manufactured to be of a size and weight that one person can place by hand but, where additional power is available, larger pieces may be used, which give potentially more stable and durable structures. This greater stability and durability is conferred by the larger weight and inertia, which increase the energy required to remove one piece and make it more resistant to natural forces such as winds and water as well as human agency.

■ Paragraph 4

There are four main techniques for achieving stable masonry:

1   Irregularly shaped and sized but generally laminar pieces are selected and placed by hand in an interlocking mass (e.g. dry stone walls).

2   Medium to large blocks are made or cut very precisely to one or a small range of interlocking sizes and assembled to a basic grid pattern either without mortar or with very thin joints (e.g. ashlar or thin-joint).

3   Small to medium units are made to normal precision in a few sizes and assembled to a basic grid pattern, and inaccuracies are taken up by use of a packing material such as mortar (e.g. normal brickwork).

4   Irregularly shaped and sized pieces are both packed apart and bonded together with adherent mortar (e.g. random rubble walls). Type (4) structures and thin-joint systems depend significantly on the mortar for their stability; all the other types rely largely on the mechanical interlocking of the pieces. Figure V.1 shows typical examples.

■ **Paragraph 5**

These descriptions are given to emphasise that most traditional masonry owes much of its strength and stability to interlocking action, weight and inertia while the mortar, when present, is not acting as a glue but as something to fill in the gaps resulting from the imperfect fitting together of the pieces. Most contemporary masonry is type (3) and although modern mortars do have an adhesive role much of the strength still derives from mass and friction between interlocking shapes; it is important to remember this in design.

(a) (b)

(c) (d)

Fig V.1   The main types of masonry: (a) dry stone wall, (b) ashlar stonework, (c) jointed brick and block work, (d) rubble masonry

(Domone and Illston, 2010: 247–248)

Paragraph	Content
Paragraph 1	
Paragraph 2	
Paragraph 3	
Paragraph 4	
Paragraph 5	

3) Does the text have a logical structure?

4) Did you find it easy to move from one paragraph to the next?

5) Which word is repeated in the first sentence of all the paragraphs? Why do you think this is?

It is clear that sentences at the beginning of a paragraph can connect both to what has gone before in the previous paragraph and to what comes next.

■ Practice Task

1) What do you understand by the term 'bioweapons'?

2) Read the following text and decide which of these sentences fits at the beginning of each paragraph, underlining any words or phrases which help you:

a) "Perhaps more importantly, the initial symptoms may not lead health care providers to suspect bioterrorism."

b) "Biological attacks have occurred throughout history and are likely to continue in the future."

c) "The biggest consequence of a bioterrorist attack may not be the physical casualties but the psychological impact."

■ Paragraph 1

Bioweapons are cheaper to produce than chemical weapons and can cause mass destruction. Several countries have established bioweapons programs for experimentation, and a number of other countries are suspected of possessing harmful biological agents. Additionally, individuals who possess knowledge of genetic engineering could alter simple biological agents to make them more virulent and resistant to antibiotics.

■ Paragraph 2

Just a few casualties, as seen in the 2001 anthrax attacks, could cause alarm. Even suspicion of a biological weapon being released could instigate mass panic and disruption of communities, health care systems, and governments.

■ **Paragraph 3**

_____

As a result, proper precautions may not be taken at first, potentially increasing the number of people exposed and infected. A few initial exposures could quickly turn into mass casualties, especially when the infection is one that can be transferred through human contact.

(Adapted from Strelkauskas *et al.*, 2010: 666)

3) How do the opening sentences of each paragraph focus the reader on the topic in that paragraph or on particular points?

4) Which opening sentence refers back to the preceding paragraph?

5) Complete the sentences to summarise the different strands of the argument developed in the text.

   a) Bioweapons constitute a real threat in today's society **as** _____

   b) **One reason** bioweapons are so dangerous **is that** they not only cause physical damage, _____

   c) **Moreover**, the effects of bioweapons can be difficult to deal with **because** _____
   _____

6 Focus on defining terminology

A coherent text is one where you guide the reader through an argument. As you do this, you will be required to define some scientific terms, often near the beginning of the text. This will aid the non-expert reader, or show an expert reader (i.e. the person assessing your work) that you understand the terminology and have considered any problems or controversies associated with it.

■ Explorative Task

1) Look again at the opening paragraph from the text on masonry and underline any expressions used to define the term 'masonry'.

Over the last three decades the term 'masonry' has been widened from its traditional meaning of structures built of natural stone to encompass all structures produced by stacking, piling or bonding together discrete chunks of rock, fired clay, concrete, etc., to form the whole.

2) Look at some more definitions and underline phrases used to give definitions.

   a) Durability can be defined as the ability of a material to remain serviceable for at least the required lifetime of the structure of which it forms a part.
   b) The term mammal encompasses a huge variety of animals, including humans.
   c) In today's scientific realm, the prefix 'nano' describes physical lengths that are on the order of a billionth of a meter long (i.e. 10^{-9} m).

3) Now check with the Study Box that follows.

STUDY BOX: USEFUL PHRASES/STRUCTURES FOR DEFINING TERMINOLOGY

A dam **is** a wall **that/which is** built across a river to stop the water from flowing, especially in order to form a lake or produce electricity.

Sharks **are a type of** fish **characterised by** a cartilaginous skeleton.

Durability **can be defined as** the ability of a material to remain serviceable for at least the required lifetime of the structure of which it forms a part.

Psychology **may be defined as** the study of the mind.

The term global warming **refers to** a general increase in global temperatures caused by increased amounts of carbon dioxide around the Earth.

The term mammal **encompasses** a huge variety of animals, including humans.

In today's scientific realm, **the** prefix 'nano' **describes** physical lengths **that** are on the order of a billionth of a meter long (i.e. 10^{-9} m).

Over the last three decades **the term** 'masonry' **has been widened from its traditional meaning of** structures built of natural stone **to encompass** all structures produced by stacking, piling or bonding together discrete chunks of rock, fired clay, concrete, etc., to form the whole.

▶   **Chapter 4** Focus on relative clauses

■ Practice Task (i)

Write definitions for the following terms, using some of the phrases in the study box, and being careful to 'add grammar' such as articles and verbs forms.

1) vitamin

2) mathematics

_____

3) solar panel

_____

4) computer virus

_____

■ Practice Task (ii)

Write some definitions for terms in your own subject, including one which has changed or is problematic.

1) _____

2) _____

3) _____

4) _____

The following reflective and review tasks will help you to consolidate your understanding of Chapter 8.

■ Reflective Task

Look back at a text you have written and reflect on the following:

1) Is there a clear structure? Have you outlined this structure at the beginning of the text?

2) What is the argument that you are making?

3) Is the text and the argument coherent, i.e. will it make sense to the reader?

4) Have you linked the different parts of the text clearly using repetition and other cohesive devices?

5) Have you defined technical terms at the right point in the text and then used these terms consistently?

■ Review Task

1) Select a long text that you have written or are in the process of writing.

2) Try to improve the text with reference to the guidance in this chapter.

In this chapter, we have looked at how writers develop coherent texts and arguments. We have examined the IMRAD structure and some typical language and discourse features associated with it. We have explored various strategies for building arguments and maintaining coherence in texts. We have also focused on ways of defining terminology clearly. In the next chapter, we will look at some of the conventions associated with scientific writing.

Sources of example texts

Dangour, A., Sakhi, K., Hayter, A., Allen, E., Lock, K. and Uauy, R. (2009) Nutritional quality of organic foods: A systematic review, *The American Society for Nutrition*, 10.3945/ajcn.2009.28041, http://ajcn.nutrition.org/content/early/2009/07/29/ajcn.2009.28041.full.pdf+html

Domone, P. and Illston, J. (eds) (2010) *Construction materials: Their nature and behaviour.* Abingdon: Spon Press, p 175.

Howard, S., Adams, J. and White, M. (2012) Nutritional content of supermarket ready meals and recipes by television chefs in the United Kingdom: Cross sectional study. *BMJ* 2012, 345, e7607.

Kuno, M. (2012) *Introductory nanoscience: Physical and chemical concepts.* Abingdon: Garland Science, p 2.

Niticharoenwong, B., Shotipruk, A., Mekasuwandumrong, O., Panpranot J. and Jongsomjit, B. (2013) Characteristics of activated carbons derived from deoiled rice bran residues. *Chemical Engineering Communications*, 200, 1309–1321.

OpenLearn. *Studying mammals: A winning design.*

Strelkauskas, A., Strelkauskas, J. and Moszyk-Strelkauskas, D. (2010) *Microbiology: A clinical approach.* Abingdon: Garland Science.

Weissenbock, N., Weiss, C., Schwammer, H. and Kratochvil, H. (2010) Thermal windows on the body surface of African elephants *(Loxodonta africana)* studied by infrared thermography. *Journal of Thermal Biology*, 35, 182–188.

References

Academic Phrasebank. Available at: www.phrasebank.manchester.ac.uk/ (accessed 18th January, 2021).

Swales, J. (1990) *Genre analysis.* Cambridge: Cambridge University Press.

CHAPTER
9

Academic and scientific conventions

> This chapter will introduce common academic and scientific conventions. Adopting these conventions will help you to be a part of your academic community, and to produce work which is clear, consistent and easy to follow.

1 Referencing conventions

In this section, we will examine the various conventions associated with referencing. It is very important to reference clearly in order to:

* acknowledge the source of information and ideas;
* allow the reader to find a source easily;
* avoid plagiarism.

■ Explorative Task

Look at the journal extracts and compare how references are presented.

■ Text A

In terms of heat regulation the largest terrestrial animal – the elephant – is a case in point. Owing to its enormous body mass, the small surface-to-volume ratio and the lack of sweat glands (Spearman, 1970; Hiley, 1975; Wright, 1984; Mariappa, 1986), elephants are confronted with unusual problems concerning heat dissipation and drying of the integument (Lillywhite and Stein, 1987). Control of skin temperature (T_s) is an extremely important mechanism in elephants' temperature regulation (Phillips and Heath, 1995) and the most important thermoregulatory organs to use this pathway are the elephants' ears. The ears of the African elephant (*Loxodonta africana*) have a large surface-to-volume ratio as well

DOI: 10.4324/9781003118572-10

as an extensive and prominent vascular supply, which predestines these organs for optimal heat dissipation (Wright, 1984). In conjunction with their great importance in thermo-regulation, the ears are frequently termed "thermal windows" (Wright, 1984; Williams, 1990). Thermal windows are body areas responsible for heat exchange. This is achieved by modifying and controlling blood flow (via vasoconstriction and vasodilation) into these areas (Sumbera *et al.*, 2007).

(Weissenbock *et al.*, 2010: 182)

■ Text B

In subtropical Hong Kong, most of the electricity consumed in commercial buildings is used for creating a thermally and visually comfortable built-environment through air con-ditioning and artificial lighting. Recent work on computer energy-simulation studies for Hong Kong revealed that air-conditioning accounts for over 50% of the total electricity consumption in commercial buildings and electric lighting comes second with 20–30% [1]. Passive solar design and daylighting, which makes use of natural light to reduce elec-tric lighting energy consumption, have long been recognized as potential energy-efficient design strategies for buildings [2,3].

(Danny *et al.*, 2007: 1199–1200)

■ Text C

The current WHO definition of health, formulated in 1948, describes health as "a state of complete physical, mental and social well-being and not merely the absence of disease or infirmity."[1] At that time this formulation was groundbreaking because of its breadth and ambition. It overcame the negative definition of health as absence of disease and included the physical, mental, and social domains. Although the definition has been criticised over the past 60 years, it has never been adapted. Criticism is now intensifying,[2-5] and as popula-tions age and the pattern of illness changes the definition may even be counterproductive.

(Huber *et al.*, 2011)

There are a number of referencing systems in use across academia and science. These systems are organised around two styles of referencing:

1) Name and date, e.g. Text A

2) Numbers, e.g. Text B and C

The name-date style of referencing is commonly referred to as the Harvard system. If your university or department uses this term, they are stipulating the use of a name-date system. They may provide their own guidelines, or they may specify use of a particular style guide.
   Two name-date system style guides commonly used in science are:

- APA (American Psychological Association).
- Chicago

A widely used number system style guide in the engineering disciplines is:

• IEEE

The Royal Society of Chemistry provides guidelines for chemists.

These style guides provide information on referencing, including in-text referencing and listing references at the end of a text. They also provide guidelines on other features of academic and scientific texts such as formatting text and the presentation of figures, tables and equations.

Whatever system you use, it is important that your references are complete, accurate and consistent. There are a number of software packages that can help you with this, such as Mendeley or Zotero. These are usually available through university libraries.

■ Reflective Task

You have now explored some of the different ways in which scientific writers apply referencing conventions. As a reader of scientific articles, it is useful for you to know about these differences. However, for you as a writer, it is important that you know how to find out about the preferred conventions within your discipline or department, and learn how to apply these in your own writing.

1) How can you find out about referencing conventions within your discipline and department?

2) Is this outlined on your departmental or school website, or on the library website?

3) Is a particular system specified? Which one?

4) Find some articles in key disciplinary journals which apply this referencing system.

2 Incorporating quotation

The use of direct quotation is relatively rare in the sciences in comparison with other academic disciplines such as those in the humanities. However, it can be useful, particularly when defining terminology. The examples discussed in this section show some common textual features associated with direct quotation, but remember to consult your style guide for specific instructions when you are writing.

■ Exploratory Task

Look through some articles in your field.

1) Can you find any examples of direct quotations?

2) Why do you think the writers have chosen to use direct quotation at this point in the text?

3) What do you notice about the way the quotations are integrated into the text?

Quotations can be incorporated into the grammar of the sentence, e.g.

> Complementary and alternative medicine (CAM) can be defined as 'diagnosis, treatment, and/or prevention which complements mainstream medicine by contributing to a common whole, by satisfying a demand not met by orthodoxy or by diversifying the conceptual frameworks of medicine'.[1]

> McDougal has also observed that the prevailing approach surrounding questions of reproductive decision-making is "based on the notion of the primacy of parental procreative liberty"
> (2005, 601).

Note that:

- the punctuation comes outside of the quotes here as they are not complete sentences;
- the page number is included in the name-date reference (usually preceded by a colon or comma).

Sometimes, you may not need to use a long string of quotation, just key phrases, e.g.

> Complementary and alternative medicine (CAM) can be defined as 'diagnosis, treatment, and/or prevention' complementing orthodox medicine. It contributes to 'a common whole' by fulfilling a need not met by traditional medicine or by 'diversifying the conceptual frameworks of medicine'.[1]

If the quotation is a full sentence, it is often introduced with a colon, e.g.

> McDougal makes the following observation: "The current approach surrounding questions of reproductive decision-making is based on the notion of the primacy of parental procreative liberty."
> (2005, 601)

Note that the punctuation comes within the quote here as it is a complete sentence.

A longer 'block quotation' is also often introduced with a colon and indented, and usually occurs without quotation marks. It may also have a different format to the rest of the text: the font size may be smaller and the line spacing reduced, as stipulated in the guidelines of the institution or publisher. The reference usually follows the quote (after the final full stop), e.g.

> Other potential risks of harm raised in the debate relate to the psychological impact on the child in knowing that he or she was selected on the basis of his or her particular characteristics (in this case, on the basis of tissue type) (see Ram 2006, 280). Stephen Wilkinson summarizes these as follows:

> There seem to be two linked but analytically separate concerns here: first, that a future child may suffer psychological harm if she finds out that she was not wanted for

herself, but as a means to save the life of a sibling; and, second, that a child conceived for this reason is likely to enjoy a less close and loving relationship with its parents.

(2010, 113)

Note from the examples given that both single and double quotation marks occur in scientific journals. Follow your style guide or the guidelines given by your department. If there are no guidelines on this, just ensure you are consistent.

Sometimes, not everything in a quote will be relevant or necessary. You can indicate that you have left something out with ellipses, in square brackets (to make it clear that it is you and not the quoted writer who is omitting something), e.g.

Complementary and alternative medicine (CAM) can be defined as 'diagnosis, treatment, and/or prevention which complements mainstream medicine [. . .] satisfying a demand not met by orthodoxy or by diversifying the conceptual frameworks of medicine'.[1]

You can also use square brackets to indicate any changes or additions you have made to the quote to make it fit in with your grammar or sense, e.g. if the actual quote is:

It is diagnosis, treatment, and/or prevention which complements mainstream medicine.

you may need to change it to:

[Complementary and alternative medicine] is diagnosis, treatment, and/or prevention which complements mainstream medicine.

If something is followed by [sic], it means that there is something in the original which is factually or grammatically incorrect.

■ Practice Task

Incorporate the quotations, in full or just using some parts, into your own sentences, and reference appropriately.

1) 'Polymers are substances that have macromolecules composed of many repeating units (known as "mers").' (Oxford Dictionary of Science, 2005: 648)

   The *Oxford Dictionary of Science* defines

   _____

2) 'The basic structure of an atom consists of a nucleus surrounded by a cloud of electrons.' (Atkins, 2013: 17)

   The structure of an atom

   _____

3) 'From Pythagoras to string theory, the desire to comprehend nature has been framed by the Platonic ideal that the world is a reflection of some perfect mathematical form.' (Smolin, 1997, in Dawkins, 2008: 363)

According to Smolin,

4) 'The period from 1950 to 1960 was truly the golden age of antibiotic discovery, as one half of the drugs commonly used today were discovered in this period.' (Davies, 2006: 287)

Davies describes the period from 1950 to 1960

3 Tables and figures

Tables and figures are a useful way of presenting information in an accessible way. The examples discussed here show some common textual features associated with tables and figures, but remember to consult your style guide for specific instructions when you are writing.

■ Exploratory Task

1) What do you notice about the way these tables and figures are labelled?

2) What expressions in the accompanying texts are used to refer directly to the tables and figures?

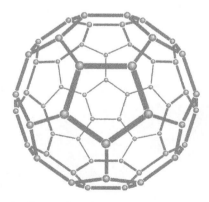

Figure 3.1 Illustration of a C_{60} molecule

C_{60} is a spherical molecule consisting of 60 carbon atoms arranged in a soccer ball shape as shown in **Figure 3.1**.

(Kuno, 2012: 30. Reprinted with the kind permission of Garland Science/Taylor and Francis LLC).

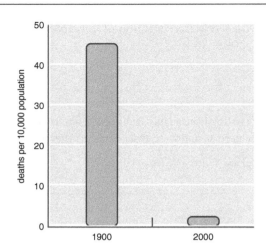

Figure 6.11 An illustration of the changes in deaths caused by infectious diseases over a century in the United States.

Health departments at the local and state levels require that doctors and hospitals report certain diseases. This type of information has been able to show how the effects of infectious diseases have changed over the years **(Figure 6.11)**.

(Strelkauska *et al.*, 2010: 111. Reprinted with the kind permission of Garland Science/Taylor and Francis LLC)

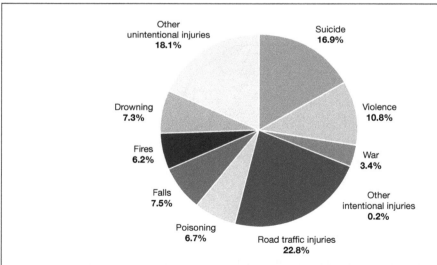

Figure 7.4 Global injury mortality by cause, 2002. Source: WHO, 2004, Fig. 2.1, p.34.

Worldwide, but especially in the developing world, injury and/or accidents are a very important, varied and growing cause of mortality and long-term disability (Figure 7.4).

(McCracken and Phillips, 2012: 175. Reprinted with the kind permission of the World Health Organisation)

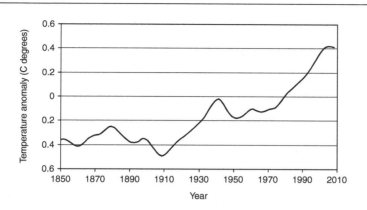

Fig. 62.3 *Global surface air temperatures since 1850 Temperature anomaly = difference from 1961-90 mean) (Climatic Research Unit, University of East Anglia, 2009).*

Global temperatures are increasing rapidly at a seemingly unprecedented rate *(Fig. 62.3)*, but it is worth noting that changes in global temperature and atmospheric carbon dioxide levels are nothing new.

(Domone and Illston, 2010: 536. Reprinted with the kind permission of the *Climatic Research Unit*)

Table 52.4 Average green moisture content of the sapwood and heartwood

Botanical name	Commercial name	Moisture content (%)	
		Heartwood	Sapwood
Hardwoods			
Betula lutea	Yellow birch	64	68
Fagus grandifolia	American beech	58	79
Ulmus americana	American elm	92	84
Softwoods			
Pseudotsuga menziesii	Douglas fir	40	116
Tsuga heterophylla	Western hemlock	93	167
Picea sitchensis	Sitka spruce	50	131

The degree of variation is illustrated for a number of softwoods and hardwoods in *Table 52.4.*

(Domone and Illston, 2010: 425)

Table 9.1 Characteristics of Gram-Positive and Gram-Negative Bacteria

Characteristic	Gram-Positive Bacteria	Gram-Negative Bacteria
Peptidoglycan	Thick layer	Thin layer
Teichoic acid	Present	Absent
Lipids	Very little	Lipopolysaccharide layer
Outer membrane	No	Yes
Toxins	Exotoxins	Endotoxins
Sensitivity to antibiotics	Very sensitive	Moderately sensitive

The difference between the Gram-positive cell wall and the Gram-negative cell wall is significant. **Table 9.1** compares the two types of cell wall.

(Strelkauska *et al.*, 2010: 160. Reprinted with the kind permission of Garland Science/Taylor and Francis LLC)

1) Tables are usually labelled at the top; figures are usually labelled at the bottom, but consult your style guide for specific guidelines.

2) Note the different types of figure (diagram, bar chart, pie chart, line graph) common in scientific texts. You may also need to make use of other types such as flow charts, and chemical drawings and schemes.

3) As you can see from the examples, there is some variation across texts regarding how titles, table headings and figure labels are formatted, though it is common to write **Table** and **Figure** in bold.

4) If the table or figure is taken from another source, it must be referenced using the appropriate system.

5) The important thing is to follow any guidelines you have been given and to be clear and consistent.

■ Practice Task (i)

Use the following words in the right form to complete the following phrases commonly used to refer to tables and figures:

show; illustrate; list; see; compare; demonstrate

1) The changes in temperature are _____ in **Table 3.8**.

2) **Figure 3** _____ the different shapes of brick available.

3) The results of the experiment can be _____ n **Table 2**.

4) The graph _____ data obtained from four donors.

5) One of the symptoms is a rash, as _____ in **Figure 10.2**.

6) **Table 2** _____ the major differences between the two cell types.

■ Practice Task (ii)

1) Complete the text accompanying the graph with the following verbs in the correct form:

    double; decline

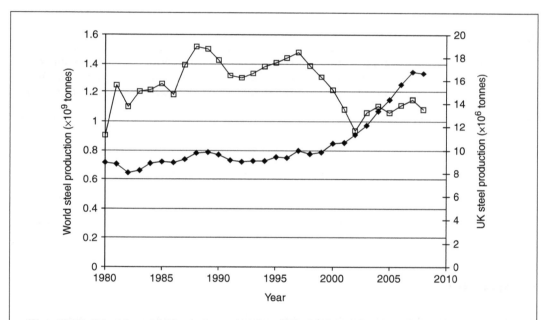

Fig. 62.5 *World and UK steel production (World Steel Association, 2009).*

World steel production nearly _____ between the mid-1990s and 2008 (Fig. 62.5), and is expected to double again by 2050, with some fluctuations due to the global economic conditions (World Steel Association, 2009). Production in the UK _____ by about 40% in the same period.

(Domone and Illston, 2010: 541. Reprinted with the kind permission of the World Steel Association)

2) Use the structures from the tables to write more sentences about the graph in 1.

Table 9.1

world/UK steel production	doubled halved rose/fell (by) increased/ decreased (by) went up/down (by) declined plummeted levelled off fluctuated	steadily sharply significantly slightly	between x and y in the same period

Table 9.2

there was	a	steady sharp significant slight	rise/fall increase/ decrease decline	In world/ UK steel production	between x and y in the same period

1) _____

2) _____

3) _____

4) _____

5) _____

4 Equations

Equations are common throughout scientific writing, and it is important to present them clearly and consistently. The examples discussed here show some common textual features associated with equations, but remember to consult your style guide for specific instructions when you are writing.

■ Explorative Task

1) What do you notice about the way these equations are introduced, formatted and referenced?

2) Which phrases in the accompanying texts are used to refer to the equations directly?

■ A

The earth's atmosphere is oxidising. Nearly all of the earth's crust consists of oxides, which indicates that this is the preferred minimum energy state for most materials. Gold and silver are the only two metals that are found in their native, unoxidised state. The general oxidising reaction can be written as:

$$M + O \rightarrow MO \tag{10.1}$$

where M is the metal and O is the oxygen.

■ B

When an element or compound burns in dioxygen to give an oxide, it is *oxidised* (equation 1.42).

$$2Mg(s) + O_2(g) \rightarrow 2MgO(s) \tag{1.42}$$

Conversely, if a metal oxide reacts with dihydrogen and is converted to the metal, then the oxide is reduced (equation 1.43).

$$CuO(s) + H_2(g) \xrightarrow{\text{Heat}} Cu(s) + H2O(g) \tag{1.43}$$

In reaction 1.42, O_2 is the *oxidising agent* and in reaction 1.43, H_2 is the *reducing agent*.

> 1) In A, the equation is integrated into the sentence ('can be written as . . . where M is the metal and O is the oxygen'). In this case, the equation is introduced with a colon, and the sentence continues after the equation (so does not begin with a capital letter). An equation can also be preceded and followed by complete sentences, as in B ('In reaction 1.42, O_2 is the *oxidising agent* and in reaction 1.43, H_2 is the *reducing agent*').
> 2) The equation is usually indented.
> 3) The equation is usually referenced on the far right of the page.
> 4) The important thing is to follow any guidelines you have been given and to be clear and consistent.

■ Practice Task

Rewrite the text with the formatting and punctuation used in the examples discussed earlier.

If a soap film is stretched across a frame with a moveable wire, the force required to hold the wire in place is $F = 2yl$ (6.1) where l is the length of the wire, y is the surface tension of the soap film/air interface and the factor 2 is introduced because the film has two surfaces.

▶   **Model Text 12, Appendix 4**

5 Units of measurement

Measurements are usually presented following the SI (Système International d'Unités). The following are used widely throughout the scientific world. Note the use or non-use of capital letters and spaces in the examples.

■ Measuring length

Table 9.3

Unit	Abbreviation	Example
Metre	m	100 m
Centimetre	cm	50 cm
Millimetre	mm	10 mm
Nanometre	nm	400 nm

■ Weighing mass

Table 9.4

Unit	Abbreviation	Example
Kilogram	kg	40 kg
Gram	g	100 g
Milligram	mg	20 mg

■ Measuring volume

Table 9.5

Unit	Abbreviation	Example
Litre	l	4 l
Millilitre	ml	20 ml
cubic metre	m^3	4 m^3

■ Other useful abbreviations

Table 9.6

Unit	Abbreviation	Used to measure	Example
degree Celsius	°C	temperature	30°C
square metre	m²	area	5 m²
Minute	min	time	25 min

■ Practice Task

Correct the mistakes in the way the measurements are written.

1) Temperatures may reach 40°c.

2) The wire measured 2mm in diameter.

3) The machine weighs 44 Kg.

4) Measure 2 ls of water.

5) 2 g of solution were added to every m3 of water.

6 Acronyms and abbreviations

Acronyms and abbreviations can be useful in academic scientific writing.

- **Acronyms** are formed using the first letter of each word in a phrase, capitalised, e.g.

  The UN (United Nations)
  The RSC (Royal Society of Chemistry)

- **Abbreviations** are formed by shortening a word, e.g.

  esp. (especially)
  etc. (from the Latin *et cetera*, meaning 'and others')

■ Reflective Task

What are some common acronyms used in the texts in your scientific discipline?

■ Explorative Task

Look at the text and complete the rule which follows about using acronyms by choosing the correct option.

The recent uptake of mobile phones has been accompanied by some concern about possible health risks.[1] In the general population, the health effects most often attributed to mobile phone use are non-specific symptoms. Excluding sensations of mild warmth, the most commonly reported symptoms are headache, burning, dizziness, fatigue, and tingling.[2] Mechanisms to explain these phenomena remain speculative, and, although the pulsing nature of 'global system for mobile communication' (GSM) signals has been suggested to be partly to blame,[3] experiments that have exposed healthy adults to GSM signals under blind conditions have not found any significant effects on the reporting of symptoms.[4]

(Rubin, 2006)

RULE FOR ACRONYM USE

When mentioning a term for the first time, use **the full term/the acronym/either** and put **the full term/the acronym/either** in brackets afterwards. After this, always use **the full/term/the acronym/either**.

■ Practice Task

Rewrite the text with correct use of acronyms.

GM foods are becoming more widely available. Many see the increased production of GM (genetically modified) crops as an important tool in the fight against world hunger. However, others are concerned by the possible effects of these foods on health.

▶   Model Text 13, Appendix 4

■ Explorative Task

Identify the abbreviations in these sentences and complete the table which follows.

1) The report recommends encouraging higher consumption of legumes, e.g. lentils and chickpeas.

2) Atmospheric nitrogen needs to be 'fixed', i.e. converted into a form that can be used by plants.

3) The chapter outlines *common* garden experiments (cf. *contrasting* garden experiments, pp. 45-7).

4) N.B. Protective clothing must be worn at all times.

Table 9.7

	Abbreviation	**Derivation**	**Meaning**
sentence 1		*exempli gratia*	
sentence 2		*id est*	
sentence 3		*confer*	
sentence 4		*nota bene*	

7 Bullet point and numbered lists

Lists with numbers or bullet points are a useful way of organising information. There is some variation in the formatting of these lists, so be sure to consult your style guide.

■ **Explorative Task**

1) What differences do you notice in the formatting of these lists?

2) How are references given?

■ A

The desired properties of a sealant are:

• a good adhesion with the joint
• low rate of hardening
• low rate of shrinkage
• permanent elasticity.

■ B

Much of the output of the construction industry comprises buildings and structures that subsequently consume vast quantities of energy for heating, lighting, maintenance etc. while in service. Over their entire lifespan, structures are responsible for (Toyne, 2007):

• 40% of the world's energy use
• 40% of the world's solid waste generation
• 40% of the world's greenhouse gas emissions
• 33% of resource use
• 12% of water use.

■ C

Significant health differences between occupational groups are found in all countries. In part these reflect the direct influences on health of workplace hazards. Depending on their particular work environment, workers may be exposed to:

- physical hazards – e.g. heat, noise, radiation, dust, vibration;
- mechanical hazards – e.g. unsafe structures, unshielded machinery;
- chemical hazards – e.g. pesticides, solvents, gases, acids, metals;
- biological hazards – e.g. bacteria, parasites, viruses;
- psycho-social hazards – e.g. stress, monotony, workforce bullying, excessively long working hours; and
- regulatory hazards – e.g. inadequate safety standards, poor enforcement frameworks.

■ D

There are four main techniques for achieving **stable** masonry:

1   Irregularly shaped and sized but generally laminar pieces are selected and placed by hand in an interlocking mass (e.g. dry stone walls).

2   Medium to large blocks are made or cut very precisely to one or a small range of interlocking sizes and assembled to a basic grid pattern either without mortar or with very thin joints (e.g. ashlar or thin-joint).

3   Small to medium units are made to normal precision in a few sizes and assembled to a basic grid pattern, and inaccuracies are taken up by use of a packing material such as mortar (e.g. normal brickwork).

4   Irregularly shaped and sized pieces are both packed apart and bonded together with adherent mortar (e.g. random rubble walls).

---

1)   The items in the list can be words or phrases which form part of the introductory sentence.

These are usually introduced with a colon, and do not usually start with a capital letter (A, B, C).

In this case, each item may be unpunctuated, except for the last one, which usually ends in a full stop as it is the end of the whole sentence (A, B).

Alternatively, the items before the last can be separated by semicolons (C).

Sometimes *and* is used to join the last two options.

2)   Items can sometimes be written as full sentences, each beginning with a capital letter and ending with a full stop (D).

These are usually preceded by a colon or a full stop.

3)   References which apply to the whole list are usually included in the introductory sentence (B).

■ Practice Task

Rewrite the following as a bullet point list.

Newton – 3 laws of motion – first law: a body continues in its state of rest of uniform motion in a straight line unless acted upon by an external force; second law: the rate of change of momentum of a body is proportional to the applied force and takes place in the direction in which the force acts; third law: for every action there is an equal and opposite reaction.

▶   Model Text 14, Appendix 4

> Note that the list can also be contained within the main text, e.g.
>
> The elephants were observed in the following defined situations: (1) indoors, (2) outdoors, and (3) return to indoors.
>
> Note the use of the colon, commas and the use of 'and' before the final item in the list.

8 UK versus US spelling

There are a number of spelling differences between UK and US English.

■ Explorative Task

1)   Add the title UK or US to these lists.

Table 9.8

A _____	B _____
colour, behaviour, labour	color, behavior, labor
centre, metre	center, meter
travelling	traveling
prioritise, stabilise	prioritize, stabilize
offence, defence, practice (noun)/practise (verb)	offense, defense, practice (noun and verb)

2)   Which US spelling is also now commonly used in the UK?

It is probably best to use the spelling system used in your country of study. Certain publications may require UK or US spelling. However, the most important thing is to be consistent, and not mix the two.

9 Formatting and presentation

It is important that any written work you submit is professional, that it is clearly presented, and has clear and consistent formatting. This will show that you have worked with care and attention to detail. It will also make your work easier to read. Your style guide or department will provide you with specific details, but some general guidelines are:

- Use a clear font such as Times New Roman;
- Use 1.5 or double spacing;
- Make titles and subtitles clear and consistent;
- Make sure new paragraphs are clearly separated by leaving a line space, indenting or both;
- Include page numbers.

The following reflective and review tasks will help you to consolidate your understanding of Chapter 9.

■ Reflective Task

1) Which of the conventions covered in this chapter are most important in your discipline?

2) Are there any other conventions that are important in your discipline?

■ Review Task

1) Select a text that you have written or are in the process of writing.

2) Try to improve the text by focusing on your use of the conventions covered in this chapter.

In this chapter, we have examined the various conventions associated with scientific writing. The final piece in the scientific writing jigsaw! Good luck on the rest of your scientific writing journey!

Sources of example texts

Atkins, P. (2013) *What is chemistry?* Oxford: Oxford University Press, p 17.

Danny, H., Li, W. and Wong, S. L. (2007) Daylighting and energy implications due to shading effects from nearby buildings. *Applied Energy*, 84, 1199–1209.

Davies, J. (2006) Where have all the antibiotics gone? *Canadian Journal of Infectious Diseases and Medical Microbiology*, 17(5), 287–290, p 287.

Dawkins, R. (ed) (2008) *The Oxford book of modern science writing.* Oxford: Oxford University Press, p 363.

Domone, P. and Illston, J. (eds) (2010) *Construction materials: Their nature and behaviour.* Abingdon: Spon Press, pp 45, 63, 247, 312.

Housecroft, C. and Constable, E. (2010) *Chemistry: An introduction to organic, inorganic and physical chemistry* (4th edition). Harlow: Pearson Education, p 43.

Huber, M., Knottnerus, J., Green, L., van der Horst, H., Jadad, A., Kromhout, D., Leonard, B., Lorig, K., Loureiro, M., van der Meek, J., Schnabel, P., Smith, R., van Weel, C. and Smid, H. (2011) How should we define health? *BMJ* 2011, 345, d4163.

Kuno, M. (2012) *Introductory nanoscience: Physical and chemical concepts.* Abingdon: Garland Science.

McCracken, K. and Phillips, D. (2012) *Global health: An introduction to current and future trends.* Abingdon: Routledge.

Oxford Dictionary of Science (2005) Oxford: Oxford University Press, p 648.

Rubin, J. (2006) Are some people sensitive to mobile phone signals? *BMJ*, 2006, 15;332(7546), 886–891.

Smith, M. (2013) The human fertilisation and embryo act 2008: Restrictions on the creation of 'saviour siblings' and the relevance of the harm principle. *New Genetics and Society*, 33(2), 154–170, p 162.

Strelkauskas, A., Strelkauskas, J. and Moszyk-Strelkauskas, D. (2010) *Microbiology: A clinical approach.* Abingdon: Garland Science.

Weissenbock, N., Weiss, C., Schwammer, H. and Kratochvil, H. (2010) Thermal windows on the body surface of African elephants *(Loxodonta africana)* studied by infrared thermography. *Journal of Thermal Biology*, 35, 182–188, p 183.

Yamashita, H., Tsukayama, H. and Sugishita, C. (2002) Popularity of complementary medicine in Japan: A telephone survey. *Complementary Therapies in Medicine*, 10, 84–93, p 84.

References

APA Style. *American Psychological Association.* Available at: https://apastyle.apa.org/ (accessed 2nd March, 2021).

Chigago Manual of Style. Available at: www.chicagomanualofstyle.org/home.html (accessed 2nd March, 2021).

IEEE Editorial Style Manuel for Authors. Available at: https://ieeeauthorcenter.ieee.org/wp-content/uploads/IEEE_Style_Manual.pdf (accessed 2nd March, 2021).

International System of Units (2006) *Bureau International des Poids et Mesures* (8th edition). Available at: www.bipm.org/utils/common/pdf/si_brochure_8_en.pdf (accessed 7th February, 2021).

Royal Society of Chemistry. *How to reference using the Royal Society of Chemistry Style.* Available at: https://edu.rsc.org/resources/how-to-reference-using-the-rsc-style/1664.article (accessed 2nd March, 2021).

Verb forms and patterns

1 Verb forms

When deciding on the correct verb form, there are three main things you need to consider:

- choice of **tense** (present; past)
- choice of **aspect** (perfect; continuous)
- choice of **voice** (active; passive)

STUDY BOX: COMMON VERB FORMS IN ACADEMIC SCIENTIFIC WRITING

1) The present is used to convey scientific facts, e.g.

   DNA **contains** genetic information.

   Much of the rain forest **is being destroyed**.

2) The present simple is also used to refer to current ideas in the literature, e.g.

   Gayle **concludes** that extended use of the vaccine in schools would greatly benefit these communities.

   There **is** general consensus on this in the literature.

3) The present perfect is often used to introduce general observations on the literature up to the present day, particularly in introductions, e.g.

   There **has been** a great deal of research on alternative medicine.

   To date, little research **has focussed** on the long-term effects of mobile phone use.

4) The past simple is used to refer to completed actions or states in the past, often combined with a specific time adverbial, e.g.

   The first lunar landing **occurred** in 1969.

This use is sometimes linked to the narration of a series of events, along with the past continuous (to give background information), and the past perfect (to refer to a point in time before the current narrative).

> The entire world **was watching** when the first humans **landed** on the moon. There **had**, of course, **been** earlier unmanned lunar missions, but the 1969 landing **was** a new milestone in space exploration.

5) The past simple passive is very commonly used to recount the methodology of scientific investigations, e.g.

> The solution **was heated** to boiling point.

> The subjects **were monitored** over a period of six months.

6) Note the tense use after 'if' in conditional sentences.

> If the structure **weakens**, the whole building **will collapse**.

> (Present tense + WILL DO refers to future time. Denotes possible events/states.)

> If people **knew** the risks, they **would not take** this drug.

> (Past tense + WOULD DO refers to present time. Denotes unlikely events/states.)

> If the government **had implemented** the safety standards earlier, more lives **would have been saved**.

> (Past perfect + WOULD HAVE DONE refers to hypothetical event/state in the past.)

Other expressions are also used with the present tense to denote future: 'until'; 'in case'; 'provided that'.

■ Practice Task (i)

Find the errors in the verb forms and correct them.

1) Water is boiling at 100 degrees Celsius.

2) Ozone found naturally in the Earth's stratosphere.

3) The World Wide Web has been invented in 1990.

4) Many different kinds of plastic were developed in recent years.

5) The effects of the drug have been showed in recent studies.

6) To date, little research is carried out on this area.

■ Practice Task (ii)

Write the verbs in the correct form.

1) The sun _____ (rise) in the east and _____ (set) in the west.

2) Pathogenic bacteria _____ (become) increasingly resistant to antibiotics.

3) In 1929, Edwin Hubble _____ (discover) that the universe (expand) _____ Hubble acknowledged that his discoveries were in many ways dependent on the work that _____ (do) by the many astronomers who came before him.

4) Since the early 1980s, developments in genetic engineering _____ (make) it possible to produce genetically modified crops.

5) In the initial study, a salt solution _____ (add) to the samples prior to centrifugation.

■ Practice Task (iii)

Write the verbs in the correct form.

1) The metal should be heated until it _____ (reach) a liquid state.

2) This type of building will not be safe if there _____ (be) an earthquake.

3) If governments _____ (implement) stricter controls on industry, carbon emissions _____ (fall), but this does not seem likely at the moment.

4) If the population _____ (vaccinate), the current measles outbreak _____ (prevent).

■ Practice Task (iv): describing processes

Complete the text with the correct form of the verbs provided, taking care to consider which of them need to be passive:

trap; heat; rely; carry; insulate; pump

Solar heating is a form of domestic or industrial heating that 1) _____ on the direct use of solar energy. The basic form of the solar heater is a thermal device in which a fluid

2) _____ by the sun's rays in a collector and 3) _____ or allowed to flow round a circuit that provides some form of heat storage and some form of auxiliary heat source for use when the sun is not shining. The simplest form of a solar collector is the flat-plate collector, in which a blackened surface covered by one or more glass plates acts like a greenhouse and 4) _____ the maximum amount of solar energy. Tubes attached to the receiving surface 5) _____ air, water, or some other fluid to which the absorbed heat is transferred. The whole panel 6) _____ at the back and can thus form part of the roof of a building.

(*Oxford Dictionary of Science*, 2005: 761)

2 Verb patterns

Many verbs require specific syntactic patterns when they occur in a sentence. See, for example, the verbs describing cause and effect in the Study Box.

STUDY BOX: CAUSE AND EFFECT: VERB PATTERNS

x causes/leads to/results in/gives rise to y

x causes y to do sth

x leads/results in y doing sth

x does y/x is done, which . . .

x does y/x is done, causing/leading to/resulting in/giving rise to/triggering . . .

■ Practice Task

Combine the following phrases and verbs to show cause and effect.

1) water pressure → wheel turns (cause)

_____

2) continued use of fossil fuels → climate change (give rise to)

_____

3) the new safety measures introduced last year → decrease in accidents (lead to)

_____

4) better technology in the future → more efficient energy production (result in)

_____

5) dirty drinking water → sickness → national health crisis (result in/trigger)

_____

Noun phrases

Whichever type of sentence you use, it will almost always have at least one subject, and possibly an object, and these almost always comprise noun phrases. A noun phrase can be just one word, or several, as shown in the following examples:

- **Research** has been conducted in this area.
- **Research funded by the government** has been conducted in this area.
- **Original research funded by the government** has been conducted in this area.

First we will look at the structure of noun phrases, and then we will discuss their role in a text.

1 Noun phrase structure

■ Explorative Task (i)

Compare the following structures. How do they differ grammatically?

1) Brown carried out some important research. The research investigated the causes of breast cancer. It was funded by the British Medical Foundation.

2) Brown's important research into the causes of breast cancer was funded by the British Medical Council.

The first one uses several subject + verb structures; the second one has only one, quite long, subject and one main verb. In this case, the second sentence flows better and is more concise than the first, which is rather repetitive. In fact, complex noun phrases are often used because they can be economical, as they allow information to be compressed. However, the choice between a subject + verb structure and a noun phrase will very much depend on the context. This will be discussed in a little more detail in the next section.

■ Explorative Task (ii)

1) Look at the breakdown of the noun phrase in the second sentence in the following table.

Table A.1

Determiner	Pre-modification	Noun	Post-modification
Brown's	Important	research	into the causes of breast cancer

2) The sentences that follow contain a number of complex noun phrases, some of which have been highlighted. Add the highlighted noun phrases to Table A.1, and make a note of the structures that can be used in the different columns. Then compare with the table which follows.

  1) Toxic chemical pollution of water resources mainly involves **agricultural and industrial contaminants**.

  2) It is estimated that two-thirds of premature deaths in adults are traceable to **behaviour that started during teenage years**, especially (notably in lower-income countries) smoking, but also other risky activities (Hammond, 2011).

  3) Tuberculosis is **a serious lower respiratory tract infection caused by *Mycobacterium tuberculosis***, an organism that is becoming more resistant to antibiotic treatment.

  4) Because blood and lymph travel to all parts of the body, they are **good ways to spread infection**.

  5) In the 19th century, Lord Kelvin proposed a thermodynamic method to specify temperature, based on the measurement of the quantity of **heat flowing between bodies** at different temperatures.

TYPICAL NOUN PHRASE CONSTRUCTIONS

Table A.2

Determiner	Pre-modification	Noun	Post-modification
articles (*a; the*) **Demonstratives** (*this; that, etc.*) **numbers and quantifiers** (*seven; several; every; some, etc.*) **possessives** (*my; his; Brown's, etc.*)	**adjectives** (e.g. *important; agricultural and industrial; serious; good*) **nouns** (e.g. *lower respiratory tract*)	**nouns used in a countable sense:** **singular** (e.g. *infection*) **plural** (e.g. *contaminants; ways*) **nouns used in an uncountable sense** (e.g. *research; behaviour; heat*)	**prepositional phrases** (e.g. *into the causes of breast cancer*) **relative clauses** (e.g. *that started during teenage years*) **participle clauses** (e.g. *caused by Mycobacterium; flowing between bodies*) **infinitive clauses** (e.g. *to spread infection*)

■ Explorative Task (iii)

Sometimes, very long noun phrases can occur in scientific writing. Find two noun phrases of more than 10 words in the text.

> Besides their random nature, the tendency of material properties to vary spatially across the structure owing to the manufacture process or history effects can significantly influence structural behaviour. Random field theory (Ghanem and Spanos 2003, Liu *et al.* 1986, Missoum 2008) has been used in previous investigations to model material field uncertainty emanating from variability in the material microstructure in different locations of a structural component (Chen *et al.* 2010, Yin *et al.* 2009).
>
> (Salehghaffari *et al.*, 2013: 1027)

Long noun phrases are fine if they are grammatical and easy to read. These noun phrases are grammatical. Do you find them easy to read? How might the authors have written these sentences differently?

STUDY BOX: FORMING ACCURATE NOUN PHRASES

1) Note that a countable noun must have a determiner if it is singular. One of the most common errors in non-native student writing is the omission of the article, or the use of a noun in the singular form when it should be in the plural, e.g.

   They proposed using completely different method. ✗

   They proposed using **a** completely different **method**. ✓

   They proposed using completely different **methods**. ✓

Many nouns can be either countable or uncountable, depending on how they are used, e.g.

   The drug was used to control **pain**.

   The patient experienced **a** sharp **pain** in the abdomen.

Plural and uncountable nouns may or may not have a determiner, depending on whether or not they are **specified** in some way. Compare:

   Plastic is a synthetic material.

   The plastic used in this product is Bakelite.

   This technique is widely used in **industry**.

   This technique is widely used in **the car industry**.

Note that in the following sentence, *which* industry must be already understood because it has been previously specified in the text:

> This technique is widely used in **the industry**.

Some terms always/usually occur with a definite article ('the UK'; 'the US'; 'the UN'; 'the sun'; 'the immune system'). Learn these and make a note of any others in your subject.

Remind yourself of these rules when you are using very common countable scientific words such as 'method', 'system', 'level', 'technique', 'experiment' and 'process'. Also, if you are using a technical term from your subject repeatedly ('molecule'; 'wire'; 'super nova'; 'dam'; 'control system'), check in the dictionary to see if it is countable, and make sure you apply the rule each time – you should soon get into the habit and do it without thinking!

2) Always make sure the verb agrees with the subject of the sentence, even when it is separated from it, e.g.

> The increasing demand for more sophisticated mobile devices are noted. ✗

> The increasing **demand** for more sophisticated devices **is** noted. ✓

3) Remember that however long your noun phrase, it is still just the subject or object of your main verb (it could be replaced with one word like *it*). Therefore, you should never place a comma between the subject noun phrase and the verb, e.g.

> Brown's important research into the causes of breast cancer, was funded by the British Medical Foundation. ✗

> Brown's important research into the causes of breast cancer was funded by the British Medical Foundation. ✓

4) Post-modifying structures can themselves be long and complex, containing clauses or phrases, including more noun phrases, e.g.

> behaviour [that started [during [teenage [years]]]]

Complex noun phrases often occur in academic scientific writing for good reason: they allow information to be compressed economically and can help develop a text (see next section). However, they need to be constructed carefully. Moreover, they are not always the right choice: sometimes it might be wiser to use a simpler **subject + verb** structure because this can often be clearer.

■ Practice Task (i)

Correct mistakes in the following sentences.

1) The proposal outlines flexible manufacturing control system suitable for chemical industries.

2) Scientist should work together to solve environmental problems.

3) The drug suppresses immune system.

4) The effect of pollution on marine mammals are examined in detail.

5) Galileo's greatest contribution to science, was his work in mechanics.

■ Practice Task (ii)

Combine these sentences together, using complex noun phrases.

1) Life expectancy in the developed world is increasing. This is partly due to improved nutrition and medical care.

   The increase in _____

2) Many believe that alternative energy sources will solve our environmental problems. Some experts dispute this.

   The belief that _____

3) The modern diet comprises a great deal of processed foods. This is bound to have serious repercussions in terms of public health.

   The fact that _____

4) We may need more energy efficient data transfer in mobile devices. The paper assesses this.

   The paper _____

5) The amount of CO_2 in the atmosphere fluctuates depending on the season. This fluctuation occurs because, in the summer, the uptake of CO_2 by plants increases.

   The seasonal _____

Think about how you could use this technique to produce a simple **paraphrase** of original sources. ▶ **Chapter 7**

2 Noun phrase use

The use of noun phrases can be instrumental in terms of how a text develops.

■ Explorative Task

Consider how the noun phrases in bold help to develop these texts and guide the reader.

■ Text A

The growth medium in some aspects of the present invention is a liquid growth medium, i.e. any medium that is suitable for microbial growth. In this specification reference, liquid means liquid according to the conventional sense of the word, and would be understood by the skilled person to mean free flowing or capable of being poured. In this context liquid media can also refer to viscous liquids, viscosified to provide easier handling and resistance to spillage from the incubation vessel in such an assay. **Such viscosity** can result from, for example, the addition of agar or other gelling agents in amounts too low to form conventional plate media. Concentrations of agar less than 0.5% should be effective in the liquid media used in the present invention.

(Turner and Burton, 2018)

■ Text B

Unless a patient needing an organ has an identical twin, there will always be immunological differences between the patient and the transplanted organ. **These differences** are immediately recognised by the recipient's immune system, and, depending on how closely the donor and recipient were matched, cause a reaction intended to destroy the transplanted organ. Consequently, transplant patients are placed on drug regimens designed to lessen the immune response against the organ to prevent rejection. **These drugs** reduce the chances of rejection by diminishing the patients' *overall* immune capability. However, this causes the patient to be more susceptible to infection.

(Strelkauskas *et al.*, 2010: 106)

■ Text C

The AI is built on algorithms that assess applicants against its database of about 25,000 pieces of facial and linguistic information. These are compiled from previous interviews of "successful hires" – those who have gone on to be good at the job. **The 350 linguistic elements** include criteria like a candidate's tone of voice, their use of passive or active words, sentence length and the speed they talk. **The thousands of facial features** analysed include brow furrowing, brow raising, the amount eyes widen or close, lip tightening, chin raising and smiling.

(Manokha, 2019)

■   Text D

Myxozoans are a diverse group of microscopic endoparasites that have been the focus of much controversy regarding their phylogenetic position. Two dramatically different hypotheses have been put forward regarding the placement of Myxozoa within Metazoa. **One hypothesis**, supported by ribosomal DNA (rDNA) data, place Myxozoa as a sister taxon to Bilateria. **The alternative hypothesis**, supported by phylogenomic data and morphology, place Myxozoa within Cnidaria. Here, we investigate **these conflicting hypotheses** and explore the effects of missing data, model choice, and inference methods, all of which can have an effect in placing highly divergent taxa.

(Evans *et al.*, 2010)

All the highlighted noun phrases serve to guide the reader by referring back to previous information and summarising it in some way. Chapter 6 discusses the use of words like 'this/these/such' as cohesive devices to refer back to 'given' information before 'new' information is provided.

The structure of noun phrases also allows for new information to be included within the noun phrase, as can be seen in Text C, where more precise figures (350, thousands) are added to break down the more general figure provided earlier. This is one way in which noun phrases can be economic: instead of using a new sentence for each new piece of information, some new information can be included in the noun phrase itself, leaving the rest of the sentence free for (usually) more important new information.

Notice how, in Text D, an evaluative word ('conflicting') has been included in the noun phrase summary. This shows how noun phrases can be used in quite a subtle way to signal attitude, interpretation and a critical perspective.

Sources of example texts

Evans, M., Holder, M., Barbeitos, M., Okamura, B. and Cartwright, P. (2010) The phylogenetic position of Myxozoa: Exploring the conflicting signals in phylogenomic and ribosomal data sets. *Molecular Biology and Evolution*, 27(12). DOI: 10.1093/molbev/msq159.

Manokha, I. (2019) Facial analysis AI is being used in job interviews – it will probably reinforce inequality. In *The Conversation*, 7th October. Available at: https://theconversation.com/facial-analysis-ai-is-being-used-in-job-interviews-it-will-probably-reinforce-inequality-124790 (accessed 30th June, 2020).

Strelkauskas, A., Strelkauskas, J. and Moszyk-Strelkauskas, D. (2010) *Microbiology: A clinical approach*. Abingdon: Garland Science.

Turner, H. J. and Burton, M. (2018) US Patent for Naphthalene derived chromogenic enzyme substrates. Patent # 10, 443, 084. *USPTO*. Available at: http://patft.uspto.gov/netacgi/nph-Parser?Sect1=PTO2&Sect2=HITOFF&p=1&u=%2Fnetahtml%2FPTO%2Fsearch-bool.html&r=1&f=G&l=50&co1=AND&d=PTXT&s1=10443084.PN.&OS=PN/10443084&RS=PN/10443084 (accessed 27th December, 2020).

Common areas of difficulty in grammar and punctuation

1 Common punctuation problems

1.1 Apostrophes

The apostrophe denotes possession. Be careful to distinguish between singular and plural nouns:

- The bridge's structure was examined. (one bridge)
- The bridges' structures were examined. (several bridges)

1.2 *it's* versus *its*

it's is the contracted form of *it is/has*:

- It's important to note the temperature.
- Note the colour of the liquid when it's cooled.

its is a possessive pronoun like *my* or his:

- When the liquid is heated, its colour changes.

> If you avoid contractions, you shouldn't need to use the apostrophe at all in this case.

1.3 Hyphens in compound adjectives

Compound adjectives are usually hyphenated when they come before a noun, but not when they come after:

- an out-of-date technology
- a technology which is out of date

1.4 Brackets

Brackets should be used sparingly as they can interrupt the flow of a text. If you do use them, be careful with punctuation. If the bracketed information is part of the sentence, it requires no specific punctuation, e.g.

- The data (collected over six months) revealed a noticeable decline in quality.

If the brackets contain a separate sentence, it should be punctuated as such:

- The data revealed a noticeable decline in quality. (All the data was collected over a six-month period.)

2 Common grammar problems

2.1 *fewer* versus *less*

fewer is used with countable nouns:

- fewer people/studies/elements

less is used with uncountable nouns:

- less time/research/energy

2.2 *a number of*

The word *number* is singular and should, strictly speaking, be followed by a singular verb, e.g.

- A number of filter samples was collected.

However, often, when the noun closest to the verb is plural, it can seem more natural to use a plural verb, e.g.

- A number of filter samples were collected.

This 'principle of proximity' (Biber *et al.*, 1999: 190) is seen by many as acceptable, but it is best to avoid it in formal writing.

Do not use *amount* with plural nouns:

- A large amount of people. ✗
- A large number of people. ✓

2.3 Data

The word *data* is technically plural (*datum* being the singular), but it is often used in an uncountable sense, e.g.

- The data shows that temperatures have increased over the last decade.

2.4 Word classes

Be careful to distinguish between nouns, verbs, adjectives and adverbs, e.g.

- Sulphur dioxide is presence in the environment. ✗
- Sulphur dioxide is **present** in the environment. ✓
- Computer programs are used to analysis samples. ✗
- Computer programs are used to **analyse** samples. ✓
- The unique characteristics of this substance, such as chemical stable, make it suitable for this application. ✗
- The unique characteristics of this substance, such as chemical **stability**, make it suitable for this application. ✓
- Nations worldwide have realised the important of reducing CO_2. ✗
- Nations worldwide have realised the **importance** of reducing CO_2. ✓

Be particularly careful with these common words:

- *emphasise/synthesise/analyse/hypothesise* (verbs)
- *emphasis/synthesis/analysis/hypothesis* (nouns)

Also, do not confuse *effect* (noun) and *affect* (verb):

- Carbon emissions have had a profound **effect** on the environment.
- Carbon emissions have profoundly **affected** the environment.

There is a verb *effect*, but it has a different meaning (to make happen, bring about), and is usually restricted to particular nouns like *change*.

- The government plans to **effect change** in the plastics industry.

2.5 Sentence patterns

Many verbs occur in fixed sentence patterns:

- They succeeded in extraction graphene from graphite. ✗
- They **succeed**ed **in** extract**ing** graphene from graphite. ✓
- They prevented the farmers plant crops in the area. ✗
- They **prevent**ed the farmers **from** plant**ing** crops in the area. ✓

Be careful to use the right sentence patterns with the following commonly used synonyms – note the use of prepositions and passive structures:

- Glass **consists of** sand plus a number of other substances.
- Glass **comprises** sand plus a number of other substances.
- Glass **is composed of** sand plus a number of other substances.
- Glass **is made up of** sand plus a number of other substances.

Note that different word classes may have different patterns:

- The study **lacks** rigour. (no preposition with verb)
- There is **a lack of** rigour in the study.

The phrase *to be lacking in* can also be used:

- The study **is lacking in** rigour.

2.6 Prepositions
Mistakes commonly occur with the following prepositions:

- a **change in** temperature (a development)
- a **change of** government (a substitution)
- the **demand for** resources
- the **reason for** the change
- the **need for** change
- **in need of** reform
- the **rationale behind** the decision
- an **increase/decrease/rise/fall (of** 2%) **in** volume

2.7 Irregular plurals
Make a note of irregular plurals common in scientific writing:

- *analysis*   *analyses*
- *antenna*   *antennae*
- *criterion*   *criteria*
- *fungus*   *fungi*
- *phenomenon*   *phenomena*
- *stimulus*   *stimuli*
- *stratum*   *strata*

Model texts

Model text 1: VLEs

Most universities **have** Virtual Learning Environments (VLEs) such as **B**lackboard and Moodle. **These** provide **an** online space for course modules where students can access **information** on course content, assessment, **and** further study. VLEs are also used for the electronic submission of assessed work, **which** enables lecturers to use software such as Turnitin to check for plagiarism in students' work. A further function of VLEs is to provide a space for students **to** enter into discussion with each other. Whilst this would appear to be an excellent opportunity for all students to develop their ide**a**s and understanding, and for non-native speakers to **practise** their language skills, it would seem that many are reluctant to engage in this type of activity. The reasons for this remain unclear.

Model text 2: paediatrics

Paediatrics is a branch of medicine that deals with the care of infants, children and adolescents up until the age of eighteen. Paediatric medicine differs from adult medicine in terms of physiology, and also in terms of individual legal status, in that children, unlike adults, are not able to make decisions for themselves.

Model text 3: copper extraction

A number of techniques are used to extract copper. These include hydrometallurgy, solvent extraction, liquid – liquid electrochemistry and electrowinning. Each of these processes is described below, with the main focus of this project being liquid – liquid electrochemistry.

Model text 4: autonomous vehicles

An autonomous vehicle is a vehicle that **is capable of** sensing its **environment** and mov**ing** with **little** human input. **These vehicles are also known as** 'self-drive cars', 'driverless cars' and even 'robocars'. Autonomous vehicles **are equipped with** a number of sensors to **monitor** the **environment**. They **are also equipped with** advanced control systems which **interpret** sensory information **in order to identify suitable** navigation paths, as well as obstacles and relevant **signage**. There has been **a great deal of** hype **surrounding** driverless cars in recent years, but progress in the field has been **somewhat** slow.

Model text 5: graphene

Graphene is the thinnest, strongest material known to science. In addition, it is more effective than copper in conducting electricity. Geim and Konstantin, the two Manchester University researchers who discovered it, were subsequently awarded the 2011 Nobel Prize in Physics. They extracted graphene, which is comprised of a flat layer of carbon atoms tightly packed into a two-dimensional honeycomb structure (Figure 1), from the common material graphite, which is used in pencil leads. The method they used to extract the graphene was somewhat unusual: they applied the common, everyday product sticky tape to remove thin strips of carbon. Initially, they obtained flakes comprised of many layers. However, each time the process was repeated, the flakes became thinner.

Model text 6: recycling

It is better to recycle products rather than disposing of them. There are two main reasons for this. Firstly, using recycled materials means that there is less need to extract raw materials from the earth. Secondly, it requires less energy to refine and process recycled materials than it does to refine and process natural resources.

Model text 7: additives and chemicals

Many foods contain chemical additives. These take the form of preservatives, artificial sweeteners, artificial flavourings, and colouring agents, all of which are added by the manufacturer during production. Chemicals are also added to the food chain in agriculture through the widespread use of fertilisers and pesticides on crops, and the provision of antibiotics and supplements for livestock. The maximum allowed levels of these chemicals are strictly controlled by law. Therefore, quality control of raw materials and commercially-manufactured foodstuffs is essential to ensure that they are not contaminated beyond regulatory levels. One technique used to perform this quality control is *high-performance liquid chromatography (HPLC)*, which is a technique used to separate, identify and quantify components in a mixture. This is used in combination with a detection system, often *ultraviolet – visible (UV – VIS) spectroscopy*.

Model text 8: nanotechnology

Nanotechnology can be defined as the understanding and control of materials at the nanoscale, i.e. at approximately 1 to 100 nanometers, where a nanometer is one billionth of a meter. The sheer scale of this can be understood if these measurements are applied to an average sheet of paper, which is approximately 100,000 nm in thickness.

The physical, chemical and biological properties of materials at the nanoscale are very different to those of atoms, molecules and materials in bulk.

The goal of nanotechnology is to exploit the unique properties of nanomaterials to enable novel applications. One promising area for these applications is medicine, where, for example, researchers are working at the nanoscale to develop new drug delivery methods.

Model text 9: carbon emissions

Whilst acknowledging that carbon dioxide emissions reached a new high in 2012, the authors (PBL Netherlands Environmental Agency, 2013) note that the actual increase in global emissions for that year was the lowest for a decade. They conclude that this decrease reflects a shift towards greener energy use.
Or:

Carbon dioxide emissions reached a new high in 2012. However, the actual increase in global emissions for that year was the lowest for a decade (PBL Netherlands Environmental Agency, 2013). This decrease appears to reflect a shift towards greener energy use (PBL Netherlands Environmental Agency, 2013).

Model text 10: the balance

Atkins (2013) argues that the birth of the balance, which brought with it the possibility of weighing things precisely, constituted a truly significant development in science, and heralded the transition from alchemy to chemistry. He attaches great importance to the fact that the balance allowed 'meaningful' numbers to be attached to matter, bringing their study into the domain of the physical sciences, where they can be subjected to rigorous quantitative analysis.

Model text 11: antibiotics

Antibiotics are a type of medication used to treat infections caused by bacteria, such as syphilis, tuberculosis, salmonella. They act by killing bacteria or slowing down their growth (Nordqvist, 2013).

The use of antibiotics began in 1929 with the discovery of penicillin. The decade following the Second World War saw the discovery and development of a number of important antibiotics, and in the 1950s, described by Davies as 'the golden age of antibiotic discovery' (2006: 287), one half of the antibiotics in common use today were discovered. Combined with improved hygiene, antibiotics have been responsible for a huge reduction in global bacterial-related morbidity and mortality (Davies, 2006).

However, increased use and misuse of these drugs in humans and animals has led to a phenomenon known as 'antibiotic resistence' (US Food and Drug Administration; Davies, 2006). This resistance develops when harmful bacteria change, thus reducing or negating the effectiveness of the antibiotics previously used to treat them (US Food and Drug Administration). The emergence of 'superbugs', such as MRSAs, in hospitals and the wider community has raised serious concerns (McCracken and Phillips, 2012: 152).

Davies notes that much recent antibiotic research has been geared towards the discovery and design of new compounds which will be effective against resistant pathogens (2006). However, deep concerns remain. Britain's most senior medical advisor, Dame Sally Davies, has warned that the rise in antibiotic resistance could 'trigger a national emergency comparable to a catastrophic terrorist attack, pandemic flu or major coastal flooding' (in Sample, 2013). She has also pointed to the threat of what she calls an 'apocalyptic scenario' in the near future, when patients could die from routine infections after surgery because of a lack of effective antibiotics to treat them (in Sample, 2013).

The aim of this essay is to assess the extent of antibiotic resistance in today's society, and to explore the possible solutions to this problem.

References

Davies, J. (2006) Where have all the antibiotics gone? *Canadian Journal of Infectious Diseases and Medical Microbiology. 17*(5), 287–290.

McCracken, K. and Phillips, D. (2012) *Global health: An introduction to current and future trends.* Abingdon: Routledge.

Nordqvist, C. (2013) What are antibiotics? How do antibiotics work? *Medical News Today*, www.medicalnewstoday.com/articles/10278.php [accessed 1st December, 2013]

Sample, I. (2013) Antibiotic-resistant diseases pose 'apocalyptic' threat, top expert says. *Guardian*, 23rd January, www.theguardian.com/society/2013/jan/23/antibiotic-resistant-diseases-apocalyptic-threat [accessed 15th January, 2014]

U.S. Food and Drug Administration, Combating antibiotic resistance. www.fda.gov/downloads/ForConsumers/ConsumerUpdates/UCM143470.pdf [accessed 2nd December, 2013]

Model text 12: equation

If a soap film is stretched across a frame with a moveable wire, the force required to hold the wire in place is:

$$F = 2yl \qquad (6.1)$$

where l is the length of the wire, y is the surface tension of the soap film/air interface and the factor 2 is introduced because the film has two surfaces.

Model text 13: GM foods

Genetically modified (GM) foods are becoming more widely available. Many see the increased production of GM crops as an important tool in the fight against world hunger. However, others are concerned by the possible effects of these foods on health.

Model text 14: Newton's three laws of motion

Newton's three laws of motion state that:

- a body continues in its state of rest of uniform motion in a straight line unless acted upon by an external force;
- the rate of change of momentum of a body is proportional to the applied force and takes place in the direction in which the force acts;
- for every action there is an equal and opposite reaction.

Answer key

CHAPTER 2: WRITING AT UNIVERSITY

2.2 Analysing the assignment

■ Practice Task (i)

Many medical devices are fitted with different kinds of alarms. Discuss how these alarms should be designed to ensure a good working environment for staff and safe healthcare for patients?

> **General topic**: medical device alarms
>
> **Focus of the assignment**: optimal design for staff and patients
>
> **Instruction words**: discuss

Outline the current plastic pollution challenge and propose possible solutions with reference to green chemistry.

> **General topic**: plastic pollution
>
> **Focus of the assignment**: green chemistry solutions
>
> **Instruction words**: outline; propose

■ Practice Task (ii)

1) i; 2) h; 3) b; 4) g; 5) a; 6) f; 7) c; 8) d; 9) e

2.5 Drafting and editing your text

■ Explorative Task

1) Text B is easier to read for most people.

2)

Text B begins with a clear contextualisation of the current 1) **situation** and clearly identifies developments in the field of 2) **mobile systems**. It introduces ideas in a 3) **logical**, step-by-step fashion. It has a clearer 4) **outline** of what is to follow in the rest of the essay. It has fewer grammatical 5) **errors** and more natural expression?

CHAPTER 3: SCIENTIFIC STYLE

1.1 Clarity and readability

■ Explorative Task

1) Text B; 2) Text A

1.2 Being concise

■ Practice Task (i) (suggested answers)

1) All the studies had limitations.

2) Scientists need to find solutions for these problems/Scientists need to solve these problems.

3) He compares the two systems.

4) In the conclusion, she reiterates the significance of the results.

5) Pollution is a global problem/Pollution is a problem throughout the world.

1.3 Being precise

■ Practice Task (i) (suggested answers)

1) The regulations cover the use of fossil fuels such as oil and gas.

2) Buildings in the city are constructed of materials such as concrete and timber.

3) In terms of applications, this polymer is very versatile.

4) There are a number of factors affecting blood pressure.

5) There are many problems associated with obesity.

■ Practice Task (ii)

1) evolved; 2) invasive; 3) determine; 4) exhibiting; 5) administer; 6) diagnostic; 7) in terms of; 8) associated with

1.4 Register

■ Practice Task

1) reckon; 2) kids; 3) loads of; 4) really difficult; 5) booze (UK); liquor (US)

2 COMPARING ACADEMIC AND NON-ACADEMIC REGISTERS IN SCIENCE

■ Explorative Task

1)

Text A: academic textbook

Housecroft, C. and Constable, E. (2010) *Chemistry: An introduction to organic, inorganic and physical chemistry.* (4th edition). Harlow: Pearson Education.

Text B: online article (news website)

Rincon, P. (2011) *How sticky tape led to the Nobel Prize. BBC*, 5th October, www.bbc.co.uk/news/science-environment-11478645

Text C: academic textbook

Strelkauskas, A., Strelkauskas, J. and Moszyk-Strelkauskas, D. (2010) *Microbiology: A clinical approach.* Abingdon: Garland Science.

Text D: popular science book

Hawking, S. and Mlodinov, L. (2011) *The grand design: New answers to the ultimate questions of life.* New York: Bantam Books.

Text E: academic journal article

Arel, E. and Önalp, A. (2012) Geotechnical properties of Adapazari silt. *Bulletin of Engineering Geology and the Environment, 71,* 709–720.

Text F: online article (popular science magazine)

Brooks, M. (2009) Rise of the robogeeks, *New Scientist*, 3rd March, www.newscientist.com/article/mg20126971.800-rise-of-the-robogeeks.html

Text G: academic journal article

Yamashita, H., Tsukayama, H. and Sugishita, C. (2002) Popularity of complementary medicine in Japan: a telephone survey. *Complementary Therapies in Medicine, 10,* 84–93.

Text H: academic journal article

Howard, S., Adams, J. and White, M. (2012) Nutritional content of supermarket ready meals and recipes by television chefs in the United Kingdom: cross sectional study. *BMJ* 2012; 345:e7607.

3 COMMON FEATURES OF ACADEMIC TEXTS

■ Explorative Task

1) a, b, f

2) c, f, g

3) examples of scientific/technical vocabulary:

proton, electron, neutron, mass, diabetes, heart disease, cancer, properties, outpatients, alterna-tive therapy, acupuncture, chiropractic, deposited, low plasticity non-plastic silts, microorganisms, sewage

4) d

5) b, e

6) c, g

■ Practice Task (i)

1) *we're talking about, spawn, cyber-nerds*

2) *it sounds like*

3) *got*

4) *bug-eyed aliens, starships*

5) *reckons*

6) *and* (at the start of a sentence)

7) use of dashes

8) verb contraction, informal tone

9) detailed biographical information in the text

10) detailed biographical information in the text

■ Practice Task (ii)

1) a; 2) b; 3) b; 4) b; 5) a; 6) b; 7) a; 8) a

■ Practice Task (iii) (suggested answers)

1) Initially, they obtained flakes consisting of many layers of graphene. However, each time the process was repeated, the flakes became thinner.

2) He believes that he has identified a key component of how humans develop mathematical ability.

3) This study aims to determine the cause of/what caused the structural damage.

4) A great deal of research has been conducted on the subject of runway friction.

5) Most thermometers are closed glass tubes containing liquids such as alcohol or mercury.

6) The solution was then heated to approximately 70°C.

7) The results of the analysis can be seen in Table 2.

8) Little is known about the proteins linked with RNA.

9) Eating disorders may cause individuals to feel tired and depressed.

10) There are three different types of volcano: active volcanoes, which erupt frequently; dormant volcanoes, which are temporarily inactive; extinct volcanoes, which are unlikely to erupt again.

CHAPTER 4: SENTENCE STRUCTURE 1

1 THE 'HEART' OF A SENTENCE: SUBJECT + VERB STRUCTURES

■ Explorative Task

1) Lime (CaO) is widely used as an ingredient in mortars, plasters and masonry.

2) One of the most noticeable trends over many decades has been shifting patterns of health and especially the causes of morbidity (illness) and mortality (death).

3) A motherboard is the major circuit board inside a computer and it holds the processor, the computer bus, the main memory and many other vital components.

4) Solar power is one facet of renewable energy, with wind and geothermal being others.

5) Although quarantine is the oldest method of dealing with communicable diseases, it is now generally used only for very severe diseases, such as cholera and yellow fever.

2.1 Forming simple sentences

■ Explorative Task

1) Temperatures rose.

2) Temperatures rose <u>steadily</u>.

   (adverb, modifying the verb)

3) <u>Average</u> temperatures <u>in the south of the country</u> rose <u>steadily</u>.

   (adjective, pre-modifying the noun; prepositional phrase, post-modifying the noun)

4) <u>In the period from 2003 to 2013,</u> average temperatures <u>in the south of the country</u> rose <u>steadily</u>.

   (prepositional phrase, modifying the sentence)

■ Practice Task

1) It **is** undoubtedly true that computational simulations should not completely replace experimentation.

2) An ICT system is a set-up **consisting of/that consists of** hardware, software, data and the people who use these things.

3) Vitamin D is important for the absorption of calcium and phosphorus by the body. It is essential for the formation and health of bones, teeth and cartilage.

2.2 Compound and complex sentences

■ Practice Task

1) Although the structure of the building was weakened, experts agreed that there was no danger of it collapsing. The structure of the building was weakened, but experts agreed that there was no danger of it collapsing.

2) The drug trial was abandoned because the side effects were considered to be too serious.

3) The panda was artificially inseminated and experts claimed that her hormone and behavioural signs indicated that she was carrying a foetus. However, changes in her behaviour suggest that she has lost the cub.

2.2.1 Forming compound sentences

■ Practice Task

1) A poor diet can lead to obesity and cause a number of health problems.

2) The hurricane destroyed a number of buildings and caused major damage to trees.

3) The drug can be taken orally or injected.

4) The Internet has improved our lives in many ways but it has brought with it a number of problems.

5) Some patients respond well to therapy but others show little improvement.

2.2.2 Forming complex sentences with subordinating conjunctions

■ Practice Task (i)

1) as; 2) whereas; 3) although; 4) in case; 5) as soon as

■ Practice Task (ii) (original sentences)

1) While it remains the case that the brain as a whole has limited powers of repair, the potential use of stem cells offers new hope for future therapy for degenerative brain diseases.

(*although* could also be used)

2) The stability of glass makes disposal difficult, as it will not readily break down.

3) The reasons for developing type 1 diabetes have not been identified, although some suggest interaction of dietary factors during pregnancy and early neonatal life.

4) Whereas chemistry reaches down into physics for its explanations, it reaches upwards into biology for many of its extraordinary applications.

(*while* could also be used)

5) It is sometimes necessary to acquire information regarding the cause of a ceramic fracture so that measures may be taken to reduce the likelihood of future incidents.

2.3.1 Participle clauses

■ Practice Task (original sentences)

1) prompting; 2) composed; 3) weighing; 4) using

2.3.2 Infinitive clauses of purpose

■ Practice Task (original sentences)

1) All structural concrete contains steel reinforcements in the form of bars or welded mesh to compensate for the low tensile strength of concrete.

2) We must understand the transmission mechanisms of infection so that we can interfere with those mechanisms to take effective public health measures.

3) Water is then added to dilute the acid to 20–30% and the mixture is again heated to 100°C for 1 hour.

4) Stemming from analytical chemistry is *forensic chemistry*, in which the techniques of analytical chemistry are used for legal purposes to track down suspects, and to analyse the scenes of crimes.

5) Aluminium-lithium alloys have been developed by the aircraft industry to reduce the weight and improve the performance of its aircraft.

2.3.3 *that*-clauses

■ Practice Task (original sentences)

1) Immunisation requires **that** we understand the immune mechanisms and **that** we design vaccines that will successfully stimulate protection.

2) One estimate suggests **that** 1.46 billion adults worldwide were overweight in 2008,[1] and projections suggest **that** by 2020 over 70% of adults in the United Kingdom and United States will be overweight.

3) It is popularly believed **that** the cells of wood are living cells, but this is certainly not the case.

4) Chemists take a great deal of interest in the rates of chemical reactions as there is little point knowing **that** they can, in principle, generate a substance in a reaction but **that** it would take a millennia to make a milligram.

5) Over time, it is becoming more apparent **that** the earth is virtually a closed system relative to its constituent materials and **that** its resources are finite.

2.4 Focus on relative clauses

■ Practice Task (i)

1) A computer virus is a program **that/which** can damage your computer.

2) Brisk walking is something **(that/which)** many doctors recommend to those **who/that** are overweight.

3) A marine engineer is someone **who/that** works with underwater equipment and systems.

4) Vitamin C, **(which** is) also known as ascorbic acid, is required by the body for the growth and repair of tissue.

5) Global warming leads to climate change, **which** will ultimately affect people all over the world.

The relative pronoun can be omitted in 2). (See brackets earlier.)
The clause in 4) can be reduced. (See brackets earlier.)

■ Practice Task (ii)

1) of; 2) in; 3) above; 4) at; 5) of, of

■ Practice Task (iii) (suggested answers)

1) Arsenic, which is an extremely toxic substance, is sometimes used as an insecticide.

2) The Royal Society, which was founded in 1660, is a self-governing fellowship of many of the world's most distinguished scientists.

3) The disease has a number of symptoms, most of which can be controlled through medication.

4) The extent to which technology can help countries to develop is unclear.

5) Gravitational wave astronomy is an emerging new field of astronomy that/which aims to use gravitational wave detectors to collect observational data about compact objects.

6) A crystal is a piece of matter whose boundaries are naturally formed planed surfaces.

7) It was Tim Berners-Lee who/that invented the Internet in 1989.

8) Fracking is a procedure whereby a solution is pumped into the earth to fracture rock and access oil and gas.

CHAPTER 5: SENTENCE STRUCTURE 2

1.1 Prepositional phrases

■ Practice Task

1) in spite of; 2) in addition to; 3) owing to; 4) throughout; 5) notwithstanding

1.2 Sentence connectors

■ Practice Task

1) consequently; 2) in contrast; 3) however; 4) subsequently; 5) on the contrary

1.3 Controlling syntax

■ Practice Task (i)

1) b; 2) d; 3) b, e; 4) a, f

■ Practice Task (ii) (suggested answers)

1) He studied computer science for a number of years. Subsequently, he did a PhD in software design.

2) Although it has been difficult for women to break into the field of science, they have been responsible for many important discoveries.

3) The water subsided quickly after the flood. However, there was still a huge amount of damage.

4) The patient was unable to sleep due to stress.

5) In addition to being very versatile, plastics are very durable.

6) While some antibacterial products kill bacteria, others only prevent them from multiplying.

7) This model of phone is very popular owing to its high degree of functionality.

■ Practice Task (iii) (some suggestions)

1)
- In spite of/despite the drug's/its high success rate, it/the drug has not been adopted on a wide scale.
- In spite of/despite the fact that the drug/it has a high success rate, it/the drug has not been adopted on a wide scale.
- The drug has not been adopted on a wide scale in spite of/despite its high success rate.
- The drug has not been adopted on a wide scale in spite of/despite the fact that it has a high success rate.
- The drug has a high success rate. In spite of/despite this, it has not been adopted on a wide scale.

2)

- The number of animal species found in these regions is declining as a result of the fact that/because huge areas of rainforest are being destroyed every day.
- Huge areas of rainforest are being destroyed every day. Because of/As a result of this, the number of animal species found in these regions is declining.

3)

- In addition to their many industrial applications, dyes are also widely used in medicine.
- Dyes have many industrial applications. In addition, they are also widely used in medicine.

2 FOCUS ON PUNCTUATION

■ Practice Task (original punctuation used)

1) Over the past two centuries, pollution has become one of the most pervasive and multi-faceted threats to human health.

2) In 1988, the Centers for Disease Control (CDC), concerned about the spread of HIV in hospitals, published a set of universal procedures requiring all medical facilities in the United States to conform to specific guidelines for patient care (Table 6.2).

3) Darwin was concerned with evolution, i.e. change over time, and he proposed a process, natural selection, that could bring about such change.

4) Chemical reactions normally occur in water, and water can also participate in reactions. (Comma could be omitted.)

5) If every individual in the world were to demand as much energy as the average person uses in North America, the global energy supply industries would require a five-fold increase in their use of primary energy sources.

6) After felling, a tree has to be processed in order to render the timber suitable for man's use.

7) The calculus of variations, which plays an important role in both pure and applied mathematics, dates from the time of Newton.

8) The computers which form the basis of those used today were mainly developed in the 1940s.

9) Scientists are able to identify parts of the brain that are specifically targeted by addictive drugs.

10) Einstein in his general theory of relativity (1915) proposed that the universe exists in four-dimensional space-time. (Commas could be used around 'in his general theory of relativity (1915)'.)

11) Aromatherapy users showed prominent characteristics: they were far more likely to be younger females, highly educated, who tend to live in urban areas.

12) The pH of the heartwood varies in different species of timber, but is generally about 4.5 to 5.5; however, in some timbers such as eucalypt, oak, and western red cedar, the pH of the heartwood can be as low as 3.0. (Commas can be omitted before 'but' and 'and'.)

3 LISTS AND PARALLEL STRUCTURES

■ Practice Task (suggested answers)

1) There are three types of rock: igneous, sedimentary and metamorphic.

2) Blood vessels can be classified into three types: arteries, which carry blood away from the heart; capillaries, which connect arteries to veins; and veins, which carry blood back to the heart.

3) Deciduous trees lose their leaves seasonally; evergreen trees maintain their green foliage all year round.

4) Western experts refer to four types of taste: sweet, salty, sour and bitter; eastern experts also include umami.

5) The trunk of a tree has three physical functions to perform: firstly, it must support the crown, a region responsible for the production not only of food, but also of seed; secondly, it must conduct the mineral solutions absorbed by the roots upwards to the crown; and thirdly it must store manufactured food (carbohydrates) until required. (Domone and Illstone, 2010: 405)

CHAPTER 6: PARAGRAPH DEVELOPMENT: THE FLOW OF IDEAS

1.1.1 Given and new information

■ Explorative Task

2)

Food additives are substances that are added to food to improve shelf-life, appearance and flavour. Two **substances** which have been added to food for centuries are vinegar and salt. Many **more additives**, both natural and artificial, are now used in modern food processing.

Geckos, harmless tropical lizards, are extremely fascinating and extraordinary animals. **They** have very sticky feet that cling to virtually any surface. **This characteristic** makes it possible for them to rapidly run up vertical walls and along the undersides of horizontal surfaces. **In fact**, a gecko can support its body mass with a single toe! The secret to **this remarkable ability** is the presence of an extremely large number of microscopically small hairs on each of their toe pads. When **these hairs** come into contact with a surface, weak forces of attraction (i.e. van der Waals forces) are established between hair molecules and molecules on the surface. The fact that **these hairs** are so small and so numerous explains why the gecko grips surfaces so tightly. To release **its grip, the gecko** simply curls up its toes, and peels **the hairs** away from **the surface**.

■ Practice Task (suggested answers)

1) Cereals are one of the most important staple foods. The major cereals of the world are wheat, rye, barley, oats, maize, rice, millet and sorghum.

2) Beer is a fermented alcoholic beverage. The main ingredients of beer are malt and hops.

3) A ligament is a resilient but flexible band of tissue that holds two or more bones together at a moveable joint. Ligaments restrain movement of bones at a joint and are therefore important in preventing dislocation.

4) Chalk is a very fine-grained white rock composed of the fossilised skeletal remains of marine plankton and consisting largely of calcium carbonate. Chalk is used to make tooth-paste and cosmetics. It is not the same thing as blackboard 'chalk', which is actually made from calcium sulphate.

1.1.2 General and specific information

■ Explorative Task

Text A: 1) b; 2) a; 3) c

Text B: 1) e; 2) a; 3) c; 4) d; 5) b

Text C: 1) b; 2) a; 3) f; 4) c; 5) e; 6) d

■ Practice Task (original texts)

Text A: 1) c; 2) a; 3) e; 4) d; 5) b

Text B: 1) d; 2) e; 3) b; 4) c; 5) f; 6) a; 7) h; 8) g

2 COHESIVE DEVICES

■ Explorative Task

2)

| 20, 21 | ellipsis |
| 22, 25, 26 | repetition |

23, 30	use of *this/that* + noun to refer back
24	linking expression
27, 28, 29	pronouns

■ Practice Task (i) (original text)

1) its; 2) it; 3) its; 4) this; 5) which

■ Practice Task (ii) (original text)

1) they; 2) omega-3; 3) it; 4) which; 5) they; 6) omega-3; 7) she; 8) omega-3

■ Practice Task (iii) (original text)

1) these new materials; 2) furthermore; 3) at this point; 4) this knowledge; 5) thus; 6) these; 7) for example

3 FOCUS ON PUNCTUATION

■ Practice Task (original text and punctuation)

An animal's survival prospects are greatly improved if the animal alters its behaviour according to its experience. Learning increases its chances of obtaining food, avoiding predators, and adjusting to other often unpredictable changes in its environment. The importance of learning in the development of behaviour was stressed particularly by US experimental psychologists, such as John B. Watson (1878–1958) and B. F. Skinner (1904–90), who studied animals under carefully controlled laboratory conditions. They demonstrated how rats and pigeons could be trained, or 'conditioned', by exposing them to stimuli in the form of food rewards or electric shocks. This work was criticised by others, notably the ethologists, who preferred to observe animals in their natural surroundings and who stressed the importance of inborn mechanisms, such as instinct, in behavioural development. A synthesis between these two once-conflicting approaches has been achieved: learning is regarded as a vital aspect of an animal's development, occurring in response to stimuli in the animal's environment, but within the constraints set by the animal's genes. Hence young animals are receptive to a wide range of stimuli but are genetically predisposed to respond to those that are more significant.

CHAPTER 7: REFERRING TO SOURCES

2 PLAGIARISM

■ Practice Task (suggested answers)

Renewable energy; the 1973 OPEC oil embargo; fossil fuels; photosynthesis in plants; chlorophyll; absorb solar radiation; charge separation

3 CRITICAL ENGAGEMENT WITH SOURCES

■ Explorative Task: reporting research

2)

a) reference to sources; use of phrases which indicate that they have identified a general consensus in the literature (*is increasingly recognised*), and assessed the credibility of the evidence (*have shown; have identified*); assertion in the final sentence that they have identified a gap in the research

b) text comprehensively referenced; expression: ***multiple** studies*

c) The last sentence indicates their own assessment of the research in the field and their identification of a gap in the research.

d) They have done a wide literature survey, assessed the studies critically and used the findings to support their argument. It is a reasoned argument.

■ Practice Task: conveying argument

1)

a) demonstrate that; b) conclude that; c) note that; d) advocate

2)

a) found that; b) supermarket ready meals; c) acknowledging; d) supermarkets; e) positive

4 STRATEGIES FOR PARAPHRASE AND SUMMARY

■ Exploratory Task: paraphrasing scientific facts

Which text	Text A	Text B	Text C
uses original sentence structure and phrasing, just retaining technical terms?	✗	✓	✓
selects particular information?	✗	✓	✓
adds some information?	✗	✓	✓
is clearly referenced?	✗	✗	✓
is an acceptable paraphrase?	✗	✗	✓

■ Practice Task: paraphrasing scientific facts

1) control; 2) 1–100; 3) meter; 4) thickness; 5) properties; 6) chemical; 7) bulk; 8) novel/new; 9) DNA

CHAPTER 8: WRITING COHERENT TEXTS AND ARGUMENTS

2.1 A simple text structure

■ Exploratory Task

1)
2. The Mechanism of Fatigue
2.2 Fatigue Crack Propagation
2.3 Final Fracture
3.1 Surface Roughness
3.3 The Effects of Treatments and Coatings

2)
opening statement
Fatigue, the tendency of a material, such as metal, to break after being subjected to cyclic loading, has been the subject of research for more than 150 years.
background/context
paragraphs 2 and 3
definitions of key terms
Fatigue, the tendency of a material, such as metal, to break after being subjected to cyclic loading

rationale behind the investigation
> *A complete solution to the problem of fatigue has not yet been discovered [1].*

purpose of the project
> *The objective of this project is to examine the process of fatigue failure in carbon steel, with a view to assessing the role of coatings in combatting this problem.*

outline of the project structure
> *It will begin by outlining the mechanism of fatigue. It will then discuss the source of fatigue, and ways of preventing it, with particular focus on the use of coatings.*

2.2 The IMRAD structure

■ Explorative Task

1)
    A
       i) d; ii) c; iii) b; iv) a; v) g; vi) e; vii) f
    B
       i) b; ii) d; iii) c; iv) a; v) f; vi) e

2) a) Method; b) Abstract; c) Introduction; d) Results and discussion; e) Conclusion

3)
Abstract – present (ref to general research)/past (ref to experiment)
Method – past
Results and discussion – present (ref to results/data)/past (discussion)
Conclusion – present (ref to paper in general)/past (ref to results)

4) past simple passive

5) *first; then; after cooling; after drying; the resulting material; the treated material*

6)
Results: *Table III shows; slightly increases when*
Discussion: *this was possible because of; that may cause*

7) *The results from this study demonstrated that*

8) *higher; while; both*

9)
Introduction – specifies problem behind the investigation
Conclusion – summarises findings/gives implications of the findings

3 BUILDING A COHERENT ARGUMENT

■ Text A

Claim	Support (the reasons for this)	Source (of evidence)
Elephants find it difficult to keep cool.	They have an enormous body mass, small surface-to-volume ratio and a lack of sweat glands.	(Spearman, 1970; Hiley, 1975; Wright, 1984; Mariappa, 1986)
The ears of an elephant are the most important organ for regulating its temperature.	They have a large surface-to-volume ratio and an extensive and prominent vascular supply, which makes the ears the optimal organ for heat dissipation.	(Wright, 1984)

owing to; which predestines

■ Text B

Statement	Premise (assumed fact behind the claim)	Support (statistical evidence)	Source
Overweight and obesity are major threats to public health globally.	Large numbers of people are overweight/obese.	One estimate suggests that 1.46 billion adults worldwide were overweight in 2008,[1] and projections suggest that by 2020 over 70% of adults in the United Kingdom and United States will be overweight.[2]	Two articles from a peer-reviewed medical journal *The Lancet*.

■ Exploratory Task (ii)

3)
  a) a <u>well-known</u> material with <u>various</u> applications on an <u>industrial scale</u>
  b) Activated carbons that are <u>currently</u> commercially available are <u>expensive</u>, <u>however</u>
  c) <u>Therefore</u>, the search for alternative low-cost bio-based materials, as well as the appropriate processes for the preparation of activated carbons from these abundant resources, <u>has become necessary</u>
  d) the search for alternative <u>low-cost bio-based materials</u>, as well as the appropriate processes for the preparation of activated carbons from these abundant resources, has become necessary

4)

processes for the preparation of activated carbons (paragraph 1)
methods for preparing the activated carbons (paragraph 2)

5)

a) 4
b)

1   physical activation

2   chemical preparation

3   combination of chemical and physical activation

4   other factors affecting characteristics of activated material

c)

the methods for preparing the activated carbons can be divided into two categories: physical activation and chemical activation.

In physical activation . . . /In chemical activation . . .

combinations of chemical activation followed by physical activation methods . . . activated carbons prepared using different types of raw materials, activation processes, types of precursors, or compositions and process conditions result in different textural and functional characteristics

6) With an explanation of how rice can be used in the preparation of activated carbons. The preceding paragraphs prepare for this by indicating the need for "alternative low-cost bio-materials" and the possibilities for combinations of raw materials and preparation methods.

7) "The characteristics of activated carbons derived from deoiled rice bran residues make rice a **promising** raw material for the **production** of activated carbon."

8)

a) Activated carbon is a useful material so we need to produce more of it.
b) As it is expensive to produce, we need to find ways of lowering the cost of production.
c) Using low-cost bio-based materials would help reduce the cost of production, so rice, as a relatively cheap biological product, might be a good alternative.
d) Different processes work differently with different materials, affecting the characteristics of the finished product. For this reason, it will be interesting to see how rice reacts.
e) Rice is abundant in Thailand. Therefore, if it turns out to be suitable for the production of deactivated carbon, there will be a plentiful supply of raw material.

9) By in-depth referencing to authoritative sources.

4 FOCUS ON THE LANGUAGE OF METHODS, RESULTS AND DISCUSSIONS

■ Practice Task (i)

1) (original text)

a) focussed; b) was observed; c) had; d) spent; e) were released; f) were fed

2)

a) to; b) at, of; c) with; d) from; e) to

3)
a) The material was cut was into 2 cm strips.
b) After cooling, the solution was mixed with 10 ml of water.
c) The alarm system was installed throughout the building and then monitored for six months.
d) To prevent corrosion, the metal was treated with a coating.
e) Post-natal surveys were conducted using email and focus groups.

■ Practice Task (ii)

1)
a) found no evidence of
b) were significantly higher/were significantly higher
c) are comparable
d) It is unlikely that
e) several strengths
f) beyond the scope of
g) there is no evidence to support

2)

specific findings based on data,	b
general findings	c
the implications of the findings,	g
the strengths of the study	e
limitations of the study	f
the need for further research	f

5 A SIMPLE STRATEGY USING REPETITION TO MAINTAIN COHERENCE THROUGH A TEXT

■ Explorative Task

2)

1) definition; 2) history; 3) basic principle; 4) main techniques; 5) technical analysis of a key point

5) The word 'masonry' is repeated, which guides the reader through the text reminding them that we are exploring a new aspect of this topic in each paragraph.

6)

- **in this wider sense** – refers directly to the more general of the two definitions given previously
- paragraphs 3 and 4 are linked by the notion of **stability**
- the list of techniques is referred back to by **type 4 structures**
- **all other types**
- paragraph 5 refers directly to the list of techniques in paragraph 4 (**these descriptions**) and is explicit about why these techniques have been described, i.e. to show that it is the physical construction of most masonry that gives it its stability, rather than the adhesive character of the mortar

7)

- These descriptions are given **to emphasise that**
- although modern mortars **do** have an adhesive role much of the strength still derives from mass and friction between interlocking shapes
- **it is important to remember this** in design

■ Practice Task

2)

1, b; 2, c; 3, a

3)

- Paragraph 1 begins with a clear topic sentence giving relevance and significance to the subject
- the first sentence in paragraph 2 is structured to give focus to the last two words (**not** the physical casualties **but** the *psychological impact*)
- in the first sentence of paragraph 3, the phrase '**more importantly**' gives a clear focus for the reader

4)

a) Perhaps **more importantly**, the initial symptoms may not lead healthcare providers to suspect bioterrorism, i.e. more importantly than the psychological and social implications mentioned in paragraph 2

5)

a) Bioweapons constitute a real threat in today's society as many people have access to them.

b) One reason bioweapons are so dangerous is that they not only cause physical damage, but can have an immense psychological impact on communities.

c) Moreover, the effects of bioweapons can be difficult to deal with because their presence can be difficult to detect, thus delaying early diagnosis and increasing exposure.

CHAPTER 9: ACADEMIC AND SCIENTIFIC CONVENTIONS

2 INCORPORATING QUOTATION

■ Practice Task (suggested answers)

1) The *Oxford Dictionary of Science* defines polymers as 'substances that have macromolecules composed of many repeating units (known as "mers")' (2005: 648).

2) The structure of an atom is comprised of 'a nucleus surrounded by a cloud of atoms' (Atkins, 2013: 17).

3) According to Smolin, 'the desire to comprehend nature has been framed by the Platonic ideal that the world is a reflection of some perfect mathematical form' (in Dawkins, 2008: 363).

4) Davies describes the period from 1950 to 1960 as 'the golden age of antibiotic discovery' (2006: 287).

3 TABLES AND FIGURES

■ Practice Task (i)

1) illustrated; 2) shows; 3) seen; 4) presents; 5) demonstrated; 6) compares

■ Practice Task (ii)

1) doubled; declined

5 UNITS OF MEASUREMENT

■ Practice Task

1) Temperatures may reach 40°C.   (capital C)

2) The wire measured 2 mm in diameter.   (space between number and unit)

3) The machine weighs 44 kg.   (no capitals)

4) Measure 2 l of water.   (no s for plural)

5) 2 g of solution were added to every m³ of water.   (superscript 3)

6 ACRONYMS AND ABBREVIATIONS

■ Explorative Task

Rule for Acronym Use

When mentioning a term for the first time, use **the full term** and put **the acronym** in brackets afterwards. After this, always use **the acronym**.

(N.B. Avoid switching from one to the other in a random fashion – it is distracting for the reader.)

■ Explorative Task (ii)

	Abbreviation	Derivation	Meaning
sentence 1	e.g.	*exempli gratia*	for example
sentence 2	i.e.	*id est*	that is to say
sentence 3	cf.	*confer*	compare and contrast*
sentence 4	N.B.	*nota bene*	Note

8 UK VERSUS US SPELLING

A: UK; B: US

Both *ise* and *ize* are used in UK spelling – but be consistent.

APPENDIX 1: VERB FORMS AND PATTERNS

1.1 Verb forms

■ Practice Task (i)

1) boils; 2) is found; 3) was invented; 4) have been developed; 5) have been shown; 6) has been carried out

■ Practice Task (ii)

1) rises, sets; 2) are becoming; 3) discovered, was expanding, had been done; 4) have made; 5) was added

■ Practice Task (iii)

1) reaches; 2) is; 3) implemented, would fall; 4) had been vaccinated, would/could have been prevented

■ Practice Task (iv): describing processes

1) relies; 2) is heated; 3) pumped; 4) traps; 5) carry; 6) is insulated

1.2 Verb patterns

■ Practice Task

1) Water pressure causes the wheel to turn.

2) Continued use of fossil fuels may give rise to climate change.

3) The safety measures introduced last year have led to a decrease in accidents.

4) Better technology in the future should result in more efficient energy production.

5) Dirty water could result in sickness, which could, in turn, trigger a national health crisis.

APPENDIX 2: NOUN PHRASES

■ Explorative Task (iii)

the tendency of material properties to vary spatially across the structure owing to the manufacture process or history effects (19 words)

material field uncertainty emanating from variability in the material microstructure in different locations of a structural component (17 words)

■ Practice Task (i)

1) The proposal outlines a flexible manufacturing control system suitable for chemical industries.

2) Scientists should work together to solve environmental problems.

3) The drug suppresses the immune system.

4) The effect of pollution on marine mammals is examined in detail.

5) Galileo's greatest contribution to science was his work in mechanics.

■ Practice Task (ii) (suggested answers)

1) The increase in life expectancy in the developed world is partly due to improved nutrition and medical care.

2) The belief that alternative energy sources will solve our environmental problems is disputed by some experts.

3) The fact that the modern diet comprises a great deal of processed foods is bound to have repercussions in terms of public health.

4) The paper assesses the possible need for more efficient data transfer in mobile devices.

5) The seasonal fluctuation in the amount of CO_2 in the atmosphere occurs because of the increase in the uptake of CO_2 by plants in summer.

Index

abbreviations: academic/scientific conventions and 155–157; measurement 155
Academic Phrasebank 125
academic/scientific conventions 142–160; acronyms and abbreviations 155–157; bullet point and numbered lists 157–159; equations 152–154; formatting and presentation 160; measurement units 154–155; overview of 142; quotation use 144–147; referencing 142–144; tables and figures 147–152; UK *vs.* US spelling 159–160
Academic Word List 16, 54
academic writing 6–7
acronyms/abbreviations, academic/scientific conventions and 155–157
answer key 2, 187–211
Arel, E. 110
arguments 103; coherent (*see* coherent texts and arguments)
Atkins, P. 115
audience of text 14–15

Badge, J. 106
Brown, N. 110
bullet point, academic/scientific conventions and 157–159
Burton, M. 15

Callister, W. 92, 99–100
cautious language 48
coherence 122; lack of 22–23; repetition to achieve text 134–138
coherent texts and arguments 122–141; building 128–132; coherence and 122; defining

terminology and 138–140; language patterns 132–134; overview of 122; repetition to achieve text coherence 134–138; text structure 122–128
cohesive devices, paragraph structure and 96–100
colons 82
commas 80–82
common phrases thru reading 118–119
common structures thru reading 118–119
communication skills, scientists and 6
complex sentences 64–67
compound sentences 59–64
concise writing 36–37, 39–40
Constable, E. 94, 112, 113
conventions *see* academic/scientific conventions
Conversation, The (blog) 14
Coxhead, A. 16
critical engagement 103; with sources 107–110
criticality, lack of 23

Dangour, A. 133
Danny, H. 143
Davies, J. 117
Dawkins, R. 108
defining relative clause 68
dictionaries 54
direct quotation: overuse 104; use 144–147
discourse, defined 2
discourse community 20–21
Domone, P. 68, 136, 149

equations 152–154
explorative tasks, described 2

Feak, C. 25–26
feedback on writing, responding to 22–23
Feliú-Mójer, M. I. 6
Feynman, R. 14
figures, academic/scientific conventions and 147–152
flow: general/specific information and 93–96; information structure and 90–93; paragraph structure and 89–96
formative feedback 22
formatting/presentation, academic/scientific conventions 160
free writing 111

general information, flow and 93–96
grammar and punctuation areas of difficulty 176–179
grammar problems 177–179
grammatical mistakes 23
Gullers, A. 6

Halliday, M. 97
hedging 48
Hofmann, A. H. 6
Housecroft, C. 94, 112, 113
Howard, S. 109–110, 129–130
Huber, M. 143

Illston, J. 68, 136, 149
IMRAD text structure 124–128
infinitive clauses 65
information structure 90–93
International Standard Classification of Education (ISCED) 1

Jaafer, A. 106

Kuno, M. 95, 107, 147

language: academic 16; defined 2; informal 16; patterns 132–134; reflective 16–17; technical 15–16; for writing in sciences 15–17
language patterns 132–134
length measurement 154

mass, weighing 154
McCracken, K. 96, 117, 148
measurement abbreviations 155
measurement units 154–155
Model Texts 180–185; additives and chemicals 182; antibiotics 183–184; autonomous vehicles 181; the balance 183; carbon emissions 182–183; copper extraction 180; equation 184; genetically modified (GM) foods 185; graphene 181; nanotechnology 182; Newton's three laws of motion 185; paediatrics 180; recycling 181; Virtual Learning Environments (VLEs) 180
Moller-Levet, C. 108
Morley, J. 125

New Scientist, The 17
Niticharoenwong, B. 126, 130
non-defining/non-restrictive clause 68
Nordqvist, C. 116
note-taking 111
noun phrases 168–174; structure 168–172; use of 173–174
numbered lists, academic/scientific conventions and 157–159

Önalp, A. 110
Oxford comma 61–62
Oxford Dictionary of Science 100

paragraph structure 89–102; cohesive devices for 96–100; flow and 89–96; overview of 89; punctuation use for 100–102
parallel structures 83–88
paraphrase strategies 111–115
participle clauses 64
patchwork approach to sources 104
PBL Netherlands Environmental Assessment Agency 114
peer-reviewed articles 28
personal pronouns 48
Phillips, D. 96, 117, 148
plagiarism 106–107
practice tasks, described 2
prepositional phrases 74–75
punctuation 79–83; for paragraph structure 100–102
punctuation problems 176–177
purpose of text 14–15

quotation 111; use in academic/scientific conventions 144–147

references: academic/scientific conventions 142–144; issues with 23; list of, compiling 33
registers: academic/non-academic comparisons of 44–46; defined 37; scientific style and 42–44

relative clauses 67–71
repetition to maintain coherence 134–138
review tasks, described 2
Royal Society of Chemistry 15
Rubin, J. 156
Rugaiya, H. 97

Sample, I. 117
science subjects, defined 1
science writing: described 7; examples 14
Scientific American 6
scientific style 36–55; academic/non-academic
    register comparisons 44–46; academic texts,
    features of 46–53; characteristics of good
    36–44; clarity and readability 37–39; concise
    39–40; defined 36; overview of 36; precise
    40–42; registers 42–44
scientific text features 12–14
scientific writing: described 6–7; examples 14
Scott, J. 106
semicolons 82
sentence connectors 75–76
sentence structure 56–88; combining ideas
    73–79; complex sentences 64–67; compound
    sentences 59–64; overview of 56, 73; parallel
    structures 83–88; prepositional phrases 74–75;
    punctuation 79–83; relative clauses 67–71;
    sentence connectors 75–76; simple sentences
    58–59; subject + verb 56–57; syntactic
    structures 76–79; types 57–71
simple sentences 58–59
simple text structure 122–124
source referencing 103–119; approaches to
    103–106; common structures/phrases thru
    reading 118–119; critical engagement and
    107–110; criticisms related to 104; overview of
    103; paraphrase/summary strategies 111–
    115; plagiarism and 106–107; synthesis and
    115–117
specific information, flow and 93–96
stance 103
Strelkauskas, A. 94, 98, 138, 148, 150
study boxes 3
style issues 23
subject + verb structures 56–57; sentence types
    57–71
subordinating conjunctions 62–63
summary strategies 111–115
summative feedback 22
support sources 23
Swales, J. 25–26, 125
syntactic structures 76–79

synthesis 111, 115–117
Système International d'Unités 154

tables, academic/scientific conventions and
    147–152
terminology, defining 138–140
texts: academic, features of 46–53; audience
    and 14–15; coherent (*see* coherent texts and
    arguments); drafting/editing 29–32; features
    of 12–14; formatting 33; proofreading 33–34;
    purpose of 14–15; types of 14
text structure 122–128; IMRAD 124–128;
    simple 122–124
themes 28–29
thesauruses 54
topic research 28

UK *vs.* US spelling 159–160
Unilife 99
units of measurement 154–155
U.S. Food and Drug Administration 116

verb forms 163–166
verb patterns 166–167
vocabulary resources 54
voice 103
volume measurement 154

Weissenbock, N. 132, 143
WHO 92
Wilkinson, S. 145–146
Woodford, P. 30
writing assignment types 21–22
writing at university 20–35; assignment
    types 21–22; discourse community and
    20–21; feedback on, responding to 22–23;
    introduction to 4; overview of 20; as
    pleasurable experience 24; process of 24–34; as
    a student 20–24; support sources 23
writing in sciences 6–18; audience and
    purpose 14–15; communication skills and 6;
    introduction to 4; language 15–17; overview
    of 6; popular science publications 17; science
    writing, described 7; scientific writing, described
    6–7; text features 12–14; text types 14; types of
    7–12
writing process 24–34; formatting text 33; for
    information/ideas 28–29; proofreading text
    33–34; reference list, compiling 33; stages of
    24–25; text, drafting/editing 29–32; topic,
    researching 28; writing assignment, analysing
    25–28

Milton Keynes UK
Ingram Content Group UK Ltd.
UKHW032213041023
429967UK00009B/59